HOW TO PROFIT FROM YO
PERSONAL EQUITY PLAN

CW00342394

HOW TO PROFIT FROM YOUR PERSONAL EQUITY PLAN

Michael Walters

SIDGWICK & JACKSON
LONDON

To Daniel and Lucy – my
personal pep packages

First published in Great Britain in 1987 by
Sidgwick & Jackson Limited
1 Tavistock Chambers, Bloomsbury Way
London WC1A 2SG

ISBN 0 283·99556 4

Phototypeset by Falcon Graphic Art Ltd
Wallington, Surrey
Printed by Adlard and Son Ltd, The Garden City Press, Letchworth, Herts

Contents

BAT . . . J. Sainsbury . . . Dee Corporation . . . Tesco . . . Coats Viyella . . . Rio Tinto-Zinc . . . Next . . . TSB . . . Glaxo . . . Wellcome . . . Cable & Wireless . . . BP . . . Guinness

Introduction

THE PEP WAY TO PROFIT

Investment should be fun. Make no mistake about it. Let no one muddle you about money. Making it can be hard, but once you have got it, using it to make more should be a rewarding experience; part of a game which can give you almost as much pleasure in the playing as you can get from spending the extra money you make.

The Personal Equity Plan (PEP) is the newest opportunity in the money game – the chance to invest up to £2,400 a year and escape tax on the income or the capital gains it generates. The Government expects at least half a million people to play in the first year, and there has been a blitz of advertising and advice on PEPs. For many would-be investors, it has all been too much. Instead of the promise of PEPs, there is a ball of confusion about which scheme offers what, how you might save £5 here, gain a modest advantage there. The complications make it appear hardly worth the candle.

Do not panic. The Personal Equity Plan is worthwhile for investors old and investors new. It can be almost as simple as you want to make it – or as sophisticated. There are PEPs on offer from some of the brightest brains in the City, companies with many years of experience in guiding the small and inexperienced investor through the share jungle. And there are PEPs to suit the sophisticate, the investor who knows how to handle shares, and wants a do-it-yourself system to make the most of the savings on offer. Whatever sort of PEP you want, there is one to suit you.

You can use a PEP yourself, and use it to advantage, with just as much or as little effort and commitment as you are ready and able to give. You do not *have* to use an expert. You do not

ix

have to have special knowledge, though common-sense and good luck are a great help. Either of them can make up for a lack of investment experience. Remember – there is no guaranteed formula for successful investment. Though they can swing the odds in their favour, even the experts get it wrong sometimes – and beginner's luck can beat them all.

This book aims to clear the confusion surrounding Personal Equity Plans, to help put the beginner and the experienced investor alike on the path to profit from the Personal Equity Plan.

Above all, the idea is to avoid becoming tangled in the web of detail cluttering the chat about Personal Equity Plans, much of it about management costs of the different schemes. Charges do matter, but not nearly as much as you might think from the acreage devoted to them in the press.

Performance is what really counts in your Personal Equity Plan. Pick the right investment, and the costs take care of themselves. Obviously it is best to avoid unduly expensive schemes. But a capital gain of 1 per cent on a £2,400 PEP would yield a profit of £24. A capital gain of 5 per cent – modest in a stock market which has more than doubled in the past three years – would yield a profit of £120. That puts charges into sharp perspective, making it clear that performance counts far more than whether the manager charges 1 per cent or 1·5 per cent, or an extra £10 to buy an extra share.

Pick the right investment, and your PEP will be a winner. Pick the wrong one, and no matter how smart you have been in saving fees, you will have lost out.

How to pick the best investment for you and your Personal Equity Plan is the theme, then, of this book. In it, the charges on the most popular schemes are discussed. The characteristics of the most common types of PEPs are debated. And there is advice on picking the sort of scheme which will suit your personal approach to investment. Above all, though, the important thing to talk about with a PEP is picking a sound, respectable manager who can be trusted – and through him getting your money into the right type of share (or unit trust or investment trust) to help you profit from your Personal Equity Plan.

Go to it – and good luck.

1 Why You should have a Personal Equity Plan

Chancellor Nigel Lawson introduced the Personal Equity Plan in his Budget of Spring 1986. He wanted to make Britain a nation of shareholders, to create a true popular capitalism in this country. That is a bold political initiative, though it has escaped major attack from the Opposition. But for a Tory Chancellor to introduce a scheme with the stated aim of adding 500,000 or more to the tally of shareholders means more than a bid simply to encourage investment in British industry – it means the possible recruitment of hundreds of thousands of voters to the cause of capitalism and private enterprise – a very Conservative notion. And that on top of the millions added to the prospective Tory voting list by the great give-away element in the share flotations of British Telecom, British Gas and British Airways.

Never mind. The privatization issues have hammered home the folly of looking a gift horse too closely in the mouth, and though the Personal Equity Plan is not a startling give-away, it is important enough for every investor to put it top of the list when it comes to cutting tax on share investment. And it is the ideal way for the new investor to dip a toe into the stock market, and gain a spread of investments.

Nigel Lawson said he was launching the PEP with the notion of encouraging individual investors to get involved in the fortunes of British industry. He wanted people to put money into shares, and take an interest in the fortunes of the companies whose shares they were buying. As near as possible, he wanted PEP investors to become direct investors in British industry, with the same rights as those who held shares before PEP was ever thought of.

Unfortunately, it has not quite worked out that way. The scheme was not thought out as carefully as it might have been, and it was cluttered up by bureaucracy as the operating rules were hammered out. In practice, the PEP does not put most new investors on an equal footing with the direct shareholder. The cost of complying with the Companies Act has meant that many managers levy extra and sometimes heavy charges for individuals to attend annual meetings. Exercising votes is difficult, and the true idea of shareholder democracy is rather thwarted by PEPs.

That said, PEPs are definitely a good thing. Disregard complaints that the tax breaks are too small to bother with. They may be modest, but for those ready to take more than a short-term view, and to build up a share portfolio with PEPs for a couple of years or more, the gains are very real and worthwhile.

THE INCOME TAX YOU SAVE

Take a simple example. Say you invest £2,400 into a PEP each year for three years, with a capital gain of 10 per cent each year – a modest target in the light of share gains in the eighties. In terms of growth of capital alone, you would have a portfolio worth £8,738 at the end of the third year. Assuming you had obtained a constant dividend yield of 4 per cent, you would have earned dividend income of just over £614 – so your investment of £7,200 would be worth £9,352 – a profit of £2,152. No tax would be payable on any of it.

Those figures are pitched – deliberately – on the cautious side. Capital gains on reinvested dividends have been ignored. You will find many PEP plan managers who project much higher results. They may be right.

Out of our £9,352, the dividend income of £614 would have attracted tax of nearly £166, assuming tax at 27 per cent, outside a PEP. It is probable that the dividend, and thus the tax saving, would have been greater. It is probable that the dividend would have been raised by 10 per cent each year.

2

It gets better. After three years it would be possible to change investment strategy. You could take the whole bundle of accumulated income and capital growth and invest all £9,352 of it in a share with a higher yield. Switch to a share with a yield of 6 per cent – a fairly modest target on a high-yielding share – and the dividend income alone on the PEP portfolio would be over £561. And that is when the virtue of exemption from income tax really comes home with a nice fat, happy thump. With tax at the standard rate of 27 per cent, the tax saving would be £151-plus that year and for every year thereafter, assuming an unchanged dividend.

The example grows more striking for those paying tax at more than standard rate. Rework the figures for someone paying tax at 60 per cent and the tax saved on dividends over the first three years is £372. After switching the whole portfolio to a share yielding 6 per cent, the tax saving would be £336 in just one year.

TAX TABLE
(Tax savings on £2,400 invested for one year)

Gross Income	Tax Rate			
	27%	45%	50%	60%
2 per cent	£12.96	£21.60	£24.00	£28.80
3 per cent	£19.44	£32.40	£36.00	£43.20
4 per cent	£25.92	£43.20	£48.00	£57.60
5 per cent	£32.40	£54.00	£60.00	£72.00
6 per cent	£38.88	£64.80	£72.00	£86.40
7 per cent	£45.36	£74.60	£84.00	£100.80
8 per cent	£51.84	£86.40	£96.00	£115.20
9 per cent	£58.32	£96.20	£108.00	£129.60
10 per cent	£64.80	£108.00	£120.00	£144.00

It is a fact, of course, that the tax savings in a PEP mean most to those who pay the most tax. That is no reason for the investor on standard rate to shy away. But the more you earn, the more important it is to take advantage of a PEP. Check the table on the previous page. It shows how much tax is saved in each tax bracket, assuming a reasonable range of dividend yields. The saving is on £2,400 invested for just one year, and ignores the chances of the dividend on the shares rising year by year, as most do. Some of these figures are quite sizeable. That is the tax you save in a PEP. And remember, dividend yields of 6 per cent or more may look high in the present climate. But a few years ago they were common. It is not long ago that Lonrho yielded over 10 per cent.

THE CAPITAL GAINS TAX YOU SAVE

All of this ignores savings on Capital Gains Tax. In most circumstances, PEP exemption from Capital Gains Tax will not count for much. In the tax year 1987–88, there is no tax on capital gains unless you realize – actually sell up and take – gains of more than £6,600. For most people, that will be more than enough. It would take prodigious good fortune to score a greater gain than that in one year on the £2,400 in your PEP.

Once again, though, we come back to the virtues of PEP for the patient investor, ready to build up a portfolio over a few years. Our example above, showing a portfolio worth £9,352 after three years of putting cash into a PEP comes back into focus again. Strike lucky and double that portfolio in one year – and in the 1980s there have been many shares which doubled or better in a year – and you would have a capital gains liability if you decided to sell. With a PEP, there is no gains tax problem.

More realistically, the Capital Gains Tax exemption in a PEP will matter more to the investor who has already accumulated a portfolio of, say, £30,000 or more. In a good year, that could easily reap gains of more than £6,600, with tax to pay. If some of that portfolio is in a PEP, however, there is an extra gains tax shelter – though not, in all honesty, a very large one. Take care of the pennies, though, and the pounds. . .

4

WHY A PEP BEATS MONEY IN THE BANK – OR A BUILDING SOCIETY

Saving tax through a PEP is one thing, and very nice, too. But is a PEP the sort of thing you should be in in the first place? Is it better than money in the bank? Or cash in the building society? The answer is Yes – so long as you set about it sensibly.

RISK MONEY

Setting about it sensibly means attending to your basic financial housekeeping first. Get the essentials right before you ponder a PEP. Any money invested in shares or in unit trusts *must* be regarded as *risk* money. It would be irresponsible to suggest that you could lose every penny of it – but that might be possible in theory, if you choose a PEP manager who breaks all of the rules, or if you pick a bunch of shares in companies which all go bust.

In practice, very few quoted companies go bust and leave shareholders with nothing – maybe four or five a year out of 7,000. Unit trusts are so strictly regulated that it is unheard of, and virtually unthinkable to suggest that one of them could collapse and leave investors with nothing.

It would be wrong, then, to say that you should only invest money you can afford to lose in a PEP, because the very worst will not happen. You will not lose the lot. But it could turn rather nasty. Prices slumped in 1975, and shares in some of our best-known companies plunged from pounds to a few pence in value. If you had bought near the top, and been forced to sell at the bottom, you could have been very nearly wiped out, even with well-known, reasonably respected companies.

Investment in the stock market is a risk business. There has been no sustained market slump since January 1975. But there have been sharp setbacks, when it would have been easy to lose a high proportion of your investment if you were unwise or unlucky. The odd big name did go bust – including the mighty Rolls-Royce aero-engine company in its original form. And

5

since unit trusts invest in shares, putting unit trusts in your PEP brings some of the risks associated with shares themselves, although the extra spread of risk afforded by unit trusts makes them more secure.

In the 1980s, everything has been coming up roses on the stock market. It has not been difficult to make money in shares, provided you have been ready to sit for a year or two through boom and temporary slump. Every setback has been succeeded by a rally, and new peaks. That pattern could continue for some time yet – but nothing lasts for ever in the investment world. The good times will surely be succeeded by bad times eventually. And when the whole market starts crashing, the best PEP manager in the world is unlikely to save your investment from losing value. Nor will you.

That is no reason to shy away from a PEP. But it is good reason to treat PEP cash as money you do not need to count on. First make sure you have enough to live on, to pay the mortgage or the rent. Then check that you and the family (if you have one) are adequately insured, and that you have proper pension arrangements. Tuck away something for that rainy day, in a bank, a building society, or National Savings. Then, and only then, see if you have something to spare to play the stock market through a PEP – cash you can take a little risk with.

Money in National Savings, the bank or the building society (provided you pick a bank of substance, or a member of the Building Societies Association) will always be there, safe and sound, whenever you need it. But leaving too much money slumbering there is bad, simply because the real value of it is under attack from inflation, and the rate of return is modest by comparison with what might be had in the stock market.

THE INFLATION ENEMY

Anyone who has been thinking about using their savings sensibly must know the score by now. Even though curbing inflation has been the major economic achievement of the Thatcher Government, and real interest rates (the percentage rate of return minus the rate of inflation) have been higher than ever in recent years, fixed interest investment has not been the best game in town. Your capital may not go down in face value, but the real value slips away month by month.

Investing on the stock market offers a real advantage when markets are rising. And though a slump may hit capital values hard over the short- to medium-term, provided you do not have to redeem your capital at the wrong time, stock market investment gives a much better overall return over the longer run.

This kind of thinking is behind the heavy promotion of middle-of-the-road unit trusts, and figures prominently in the literature from many PEP schemes. Pick what figures you like from whatever period you choose. The following example found in the PEP brochure from leading unit trust group Save & Prosper accurately gives the flavour of how it works.

Save & Prosper calculates that £2,400 invested from 1 January 1976 to 1 November 1986 would be worth £6,157 in a building society, with all income reinvested. Put into shares which tracked the performance of the *Financial Times* All-share Index (the broad stock market average) over the same period, £2,400 would have grown to £14,190, all income reinvested, with no liability to Capital Gains Tax (a reasonable assumption).

Other brochures yield variations on the same theme. No matter how you calculate it, they all demonstrate clearly that investment in shares is a much better deal – long-term – than cash in the National Savings Bank, a High Street bank, or a building society. The Save & Prosper example goes on to show that, with the tax exemption of a PEP, the £2,400 would have grown to £17,532 over the same period – an extra £3,342 by comparison with share investment without a PEP. Once again, the message is clear: PEP tax concessions may not appear wonderful over a short run, but give them a longer spin and they really are worthwhile.

One note of warning. Almost all of the examples in unit trust and PEP promotional literature cover a period which starts after January 1975, when the *Financial Times* Ordinary Share Index slumped to what now looks a freak low of 146. By the Spring of 1987, it had multiplied ten-fold. So comparisons running back ten years or more are truthful, but tend to look unduly flattering set against building society investments. In future, the share gains are unlikely to be as bright as in the past decade – but over most periods longer than three or four years, there is still a significant plus in shares. Remember, though, you pay for that plus by taking the risk that your capital value can fall as well as rise.

While we are picking holes, it is worth noticing that some comparisons do not always play quite fair. It is not always clear how Capital Gains Tax liabilities are calculated, and figures showing how you would have fared without a PEP sometimes seem to be understated. Nevertheless, the message is still loud and clear – you make more money with a PEP.

THE IDEAL WAY INTO THE STOCK MARKET

So long as you understand that a PEP takes you into the share jungle, and that the jungle can be dangerous, a PEP is pretty nearly the ideal way in. It ought to be simple (we look at the mechanics in the next chapter), it ought to be fairly safe; it can give you a good spread of investments under expert management, it does not involve risking an enormous amount of money; and it carries very useful tax savings – and the unique advantage of being secure from the prying eyes of the Inland Revenue.

ESPECIALLY FOR THE LADIES

There is no requirement to tell the tax man about your PEP. That gives it a very special advantage over other forms of investment for married women who want to handle their own financial affairs – privately. There are all sorts of reasons why married women might prefer to build up a nest-egg without involving their husbands. Most are thwarted by the absurdity of a tax system which holds the husband responsible for reporting most of his wife's tax affairs. Even if the wife opts for the earnings election, which makes her earned income her responsibility, and not part of her husband's income for tax purposes, any investment income earned by the wife still has to be taxed as part of her husband's income, and revealed to her husband to disclose on his tax return. You cannot dodge it. I got a nasty letter from my tax inspector because my wife had a few hundred pounds earning interest in a bank account she had forgotten.

It is daft, of course. And there may be very good tax reasons why the wife's earnings election is not suitable for many married couples. But because a PEP does not need to be reported to the tax man it allows a wife some freedom to run a totally independent, if modest, investment portfolio of her own.

DOUBLE YOUR PEP MONEY

The other side of that coin is the opportunity for each family to double their PEP money each year, should they wish. For both husband and wife can run a PEP. Anyone over the age of eighteen can have one. So many families can shelter £4,800 a year from tax.

Though the two PEP portfolios may be separate in theory, in practice, for most couples, this concession to a woman's financial independence merely doubles the fun. Once again, the tax savings emerge as more valuable than many have realized. Go back to our earlier examples of the tax savings on dividend income, and double them.

So take no notice of those who say the PEP is not worth the bother. The savings are real, and a PEP ought to be essential for anyone paying tax at higher rates. The advantages of PEPs are there for the taking, a bonus for anyone who intends to invest in shares or unit trusts. Make the most of them.

2 The Way the PEP Works

The Personal Equity Plan ought to have been a simple, straightforward way of encouraging investors to buy shares in British industry, sit with them, take an interest in their affairs, and be suitably rewarded with tax-free interest and capital gains for their pains.

It has not worked out that way. The theory was simple, but the practice is trickier. The detailed rules are tedious and more complicated than they need be. The cost of running the scheme has prompted plan managers to introduce further complications, and sometimes to devise a tangled thread of charges. Do not weaken. It is worth being aware of the rules, but once your PEP is up and running, it should go fairly smoothly.

WHO CAN PLAY

Any British taxpayer over the age of eighteen can have one PEP each year. If you work overseas, check with your tax office. You may be allowed one. There is no restriction on the number of PEPs in each household.

HOW MUCH

Up to £2,400 is allowed into each PEP, each year. The cash allowance cannot be split between different PEPs, and if you put in less than £2,400 in one year, you cannot transfer any of the unused allowance into the next year. The chance is gone. There is no minimum investment, though under £100 would be impractical because too much would be gobbled up in charges.

HOW LONG

Capital gains on the investment, or income from it, are free of tax so long as the money remains in each PEP for at least one full calendar year – that means for the whole of 1988 if you start a PEP during 1987. You have to be in by 1 January 1988 and still be there on 31 December 1988. If you start a PEP in 1988, the money must stay in for the whole of 1989, and so on. This means there is no tax disadvantage in starting your first PEP on 31 December 1987, instead of earlier in 1987.

Even if you had started on 1 January 1987, you could not have taken any money out before 1 January 1989 without losing the tax concessions, although the early starter will have had the chance of tax-free capital gains during 1987. The money can, however, be withdrawn at any time. Early withdrawal simply means you pay your normal rate of tax on any dividends, and Capital Gains Tax at the normal 30 per cent rate in the less likely event of any being due. The shortest period you can use a PEP for is a year and a day, but that year has to be a calendar year – a pointless and fiddlesome complication.

WHAT YOU CAN PUT INTO YOUR PEP

Most of the money in a PEP must be invested in the stock market for most of the time. But if you put in £2,399 or less, it can go into an account which earns high interest, where it can stay until 28 January of the following year – a useful option in times of share market uncertainty.

Once you put up the full £2,400, it must be invested within 28 days or by 31 December of that year, whichever comes first.

As soon as you have made your first investment, you are not allowed to hold cash equal to more than 10 per cent of the PEP's value at the end of the previous calendar year, or more than £240, whichever is the greater.

Chancellor Nigel Lawson's intention was to restrict PEPs to shares, but he weakened. So you can put up to £35 a month or a lump sum of up to £420 into unit trusts or investment trusts, or up to 25 per cent of your total investment, whichever is the

11

greater. That means, if you put the full £2,400 into a PEP, a maximum of £600 or £50 a month can go into unit trusts or investment trusts.

The £35 monthly concession has made room for PEPs which offer only a modest monthly investment in unit trusts. Once you have put money into shares, that part of the money cannot be switched into unit trusts or investment trusts.

Shares in UK public companies quoted on the Stock Exchange or on the Unlisted Securities Market qualify. Shares traded on the Stock Exchange Third Market, on the Over-The-Counter Market, or on markets overseas do not. You can get overseas exposure by using the unit trust and investment trust allowances to buy UK-based trusts specializing in foreign shares.

WHO CAN RUN IT

The PEP has to be run through a plan manager – which forces a middle-man into the picture, deprives the experienced investor of the opportunity of doing exactly what he wishes, and adds a layer of costs. But it does ensure that there are experienced investment houses on hand to take care of the less sophisticated player, offering PEPs with a good degree of security and skill.

Plan managers must be authorized to deal in securities, and must have a registration certificate from the Inland Revenue. In practice, they will all fall eventually into the self-regulation system being set in motion by the Financial Services Act, and controlled by the Securities & Investment Board (SIB) headed by Sir Kenneth Berrill.

Within that framework, each manager will be responsible to the agency which covers his own area of operation. The High Street banks all have PEPs on offer. So do many unit trust groups, stockbrokers, and some building societies and investment trusts. Many investment advisers are also in on the act. They should belong to FIMBRA, the Financial Intermediaries, Managers & Brokers Regulatory Association. Most will display the FIMBRA name in their advertising, but you can check if they are members by contacting FIMBRA at 22, Great Tower Street, London EC3R 5AQ. Telephone: 01–929 2711.

It is important to deal with names you can trust. The big banks, members of the Stock Exchange, building societies and investment trusts all have clearly understood and established standards of practice, and well-tried supervision. They may not always offer the best and most efficient service, but they belong to a system which guarantees standards of integrity – or clear compensation should they lapse.

FIMBRA membership is more of a puzzle. When the system is working properly, it will offer a good degree of protection, and a compensation fund for anyone defrauded or treated unfairly. It may be well into 1988 before it is organized properly, and even longer before it is working as well as everyone would wish. So be careful. FIMBRA membership will not be a complete guarantee against problems every time.

There is a chance, too, that until well into 1988 some PEPs will be on offer from people who do not belong to FIMBRA or any other part of the SIB set-up. These operators may be in dispute with FIMBRA, and may or may not eventually gain membership of some appropriate regulatory authority. If they are kept out, they will be forced out of the investment advice business, probably before the end of 1988. If there is any question of this, stay away. You have no need to take chances. There are plenty of safe and sound managers to choose from.

THE PAPERWORK

Sensibly enough, there are tight rules governing how the managers handle your money. All deals should be done at open-market prices, and all investors should be sent full details of any purchases or sales made for them. Some managers send contract notes with a brief explanation of why each individual share has been bought.

The managers can – and most do – pool thousands of individual names together when they buy them all shares in the same company, and that interest will appear on the company's share register in the plan manager's nominee name, not the

13

name of the individual PEP holder. Each investor, however, will have clear title to their shares. Any cash in the plan must go into a special deposit account which pays interest before the deduction of tax. It cannot be mixed with the manager's own money.

Deal with a reputable plan manager, and you can be confident that such basic investment housekeeping will be carried out properly, with your interests in mind. There should be no need to worry about the paperwork.

HOW YOU CAN MOVE YOUR INVESTMENTS

Unfortunately, you cannot simply shunt shares you already hold into your PEP. Purchases must go through your PEP manager, so if you want to put one of your old favourites in, you have to sell it, and get the manager to repurchase an equivalent amount for your PEP. For the established investor, that is a bore, but it closes an obvious tax-saving loophole.

Once your cash is in, however, you are free to move investments around within the PEP as much as you like – though the plan manager may charge for most changes, and it can be expensive if you play around too much. There are no tax complications on switching, so long as the cash stays within the original PEP framework. Remember, though, that it is not possible to switch between shares and unit or investment trusts once you have made your first choice.

TAKING AN INCOME

Taking income from your PEP is not possible until the plan has matured, but then this becomes a very attractive proposition. All dividends and interest have to be reinvested within the PEP, and if they are taken out in the qualifying year, the whole plan is void. Once the plan is mature, dividends cannot be taken out directly, or they are taxed. However, there is nothing to stop holders withdrawing a regular amount from a mature plan as frequently as they choose. So once a reasonable amount of capital and income has been accumulated in a mature plan, it can serve as an excellent source of tax-free income. That is a big bonus, and one which has been widely overlooked.

CHANGING MANAGERS

You can change PEP managers in mid-stream. The problem is cost. In addition to the initial management charges incurred with each new manager, there could be extra termination and transfer costs as you move out of your old scheme. So best make sure you pick the right manager first time.

3 What Your Pep Should Cost

Sorting out charges for PEPs is the real passion-killer. Look at the obsessive interest in charges in the press and you will end up tearing out your hair. The variations are infinite, with different managers charging different amounts for different facilities, and with new schemes appearing all the while.

Accept that you will probably only manage to pick the cheapest scheme by luck. So much depends on just how you want to use your PEP, and you may not discover that until your PEP is up and running. So do not get swamped by the detail of the various charges. Simply try to ensure that you avoid the most expensive, and concentrate on picking the most reputable manager and the one whose ideas suit you best. Once again, it is worth emphasizing that saving a few pounds on expenses matters much less than choosing the right investments.

Unfortunately, there are several different points at which costs can be incurred. Not all PEPs levy charges at all of these points, and sometimes the absence of charges for one facility is covered by higher charges for another.

THE INITIAL CHARGE

Most PEPs make a charge for opening the plan. It is a once-and-for-all payment, not repeated each year that you hold the plan. If, however, you put money into a PEP each year, there is an initial charge on that new money, since each year's PEP payment is treated as the start of a new plan, not as a continuation of the existing one. All charges attract Value

Added Tax, a modest extra irritant. In comparing costs, the VAT levy has not been taken into account.

The highest initial charge in most plans is 5 per cent. Many of the PEPs which levy it are based on the plan produced by Fidelity, a well-respected unit trust management group, which was the first to take up PEPs with enthusiasm. Other companies have slapped their own name on to the Fidelity scheme – including the Abbey National Building Society, and investment advisers Hargreaves Lansdown.

Others with a 5 per cent initial charge include Bradford & Bingley Building Society, F. S. Investment Managers, merchant bankers Hill Samuel and N. M. Schroder, and unit trust groups Gartmore and MIM Britannia. Unless there are compensating reductions in other charges, this looks on the high side. On a full £2,400 investment, the 5 per cent equals a hefty £120. Would-be investors should only accept it if they are confident that the investment performance will be above-average, or if plans from these organizations have features which are of particular appeal. As we will see in the detailed analysis of individual plans, the Fidelity schemes cosset you in an effort to earn their corn.

The full range of initial charges goes down from 5 per cent to nil on some plans including those from the Midland Bank, Bank of Scotland and the Yorkshire Bank, and insurance companies Equitable Life and the Prudential. Others make a fixed sum entry charge, commonly between £50 and £25. Whereas £50 looks much lower than 5 per cent, the real size of a fixed entry fee depends on how much you are investing. If you are only putting £500 in, then £50 is a 10 per cent initial fee. So check first.

THE ANNUAL CHARGE

Every one of the first 100 or so schemes levied an annual charge, and it is unlikely that any PEPs will appear without one. The annual charge is bread and butter to investment managers. They all hope to see their clients prosper and, quite properly, to reap a steadily rising annual charge as the value of their clients' investments goes up.

17

The highest annual charges appear to have settled at 2 per cent or so, though F.S., the Scots investment managers, are levying 2·4 per cent on their rather specialist plan, which is aimed at sophisticated investors. Equitable Life wants 2·5 per cent for the first two years, with a subsequent reduction to 1 per cent, but levies no initial charge. The Bank of Scotland is making up for the absence of an initial charge with a relatively high 2 per cent annual fee on most plans, and so is the Prudential. The Pru, however, will not actually bill you for the annual charge until the end of the first two years.

Other annual charges go down to the 0·75 per cent from stockbrokers Rensburg, and certainly no one should object to charges in the 1 to 1·5 per cent range, other features being equal.

DEALING CHARGES

Everyone has to pay a dealing charge almost every time they buy or sell shares, something which is often forgotten by commentators who compare PEP charges with other investments. Since the Big Bang in October 1986, share dealing commissions have not been fixed. Some PEP managers are giving investors a bargain on dealing costs, perhaps to compensate for heavier fees elsewhere in their packages. Others take a comparatively fat margin.

The old Stock Exchange commission used to be 1·65 per cent for smaller deals, with a minimum charge of around £15 for the kind of small deals which might well be done by a PEP holder.

On the face of it, some PEP managers are providing an absolutely first-class service; some charging nothing at all for dealing, others as little as 0·2 per cent. This comes about because some managers buy only a limited range of shares, and lump together all individual purchases to buy a large number of shares at a time, using their muscle to secure a low commission rate which they pass on to their individual clients. Excellent.

Bradford & Bingley Building Society, which has one of the highest initial charges, makes no charge for dealing. Nor do bankers Hill Samuel, another with a 5 per cent initial charge.

The relatively expensive Fidelity schemes confine dealing costs to between 0·2 per cent and 0·5 per cent.

Among the heaviest of the dealing costs is 1·65 per cent by stockbrokers Alexanders Laing & Cruickshank and Laurence Keen. But both have initial and annual charges at the lower end of the scale.

STAMP DUTY

Stamp duty is inescapable for the conventional share buyer. There is a standard Government levy of 0·5 per cent on any purchase. Most PEP managers simply pass it on, but not all. Bradford & Bingley absorbs it in its annual charge.

WITHDRAWAL CHARGES

Just as normal investors pay a commission to sell shares, some PEP investors must pay to get their money back. Once again, though, many managers offer a good deal, making no charge for withdrawal at any time. These include those operating the Fidelity scheme, and Broker Financial Services, Equitable Life, stockbrokers Kleinwort Grieveson, investment advisers Lamont & Partners, Lloyds Bank and Yorkshire Bank, unit trust experts M & G and MIM Britannia and the Prudential, and bankers N. M. Schroder.

Other managers charge nothing for withdrawing once the PEP has run at least a year and a day, and has matured, confining charges to those who opt out early. National Westminster Bank has one of the heaviest get-out charges, a fee of £25 for those leaving within the first two mature years. Brokers Laurence Keen charge £40 on withdrawal.

UNIT TRUST CHARGES

If you choose a PEP which includes a stake in a unit trust, there are further refinements on the charging scale. The thing to

19

dodge is double-charging. Most of the main groups avoid this, or offer some reduction in the 5 per cent front-end loan which you incur when buying unit trusts.

OTHER CHARGES

Lest you wilt beneath the onslaught of this ever-extending list of costs, be reassured that the remaining charges can be regarded as optional extras, to be paid by the keenest PEP punters only. Or by those who did not look carefully enough to start with, and later made moves they had not thought they would make when they started.

Where you are allowed to buy extra shares outside your initial list, some managers charge £5 or £10 a share.

When you wish to attend the annual meeting of any company you have invested in, most schemes also make an extra charge. The mechanics of PEPs are such that this elementary right involves additional paperwork for the managers. Among the cheapest fees is £5 a meeting from Lloyds Bank and Yorkshire Bank. Others charge £10. Some – like MIM Britannia – charge £35 a year or more; while others seek a hefty £25 a meeting, ranging up to a prohibitive £50 from Bradford & Bingley. Some positively discourage investors from going to meetings.

Attendance is one thing, while exercising votes and speaking may be yet another. National Westminster Bank charges £100 a year to secure you full shareholders rights, with no charge for simply attending meetings.

The idea of extra charges for doing what proper shareholders can do as of right runs counter to the original idea of PEPs, and the Chancellor really ought to use his muscle to see that PEP legislation eliminates them.

He should also act to ensure that all public companies agree to supply their annual report and all other shareholder litera-ture direct to any individual PEP investors who want it, without charge to investors or PEP managers.

Behind the scenes, there has been a row over who pays for the supply of printed matter, and this has bumped up charges to PEP investors because many leading companies have in-sisted that PEP managers pay some or all of the costs of distributing reports. This short-sighted view runs directly against ideas of encouraging individual interest in industry.

It has also restricted investor choice. While not all of them will admit it, some managers are only allowing PEP holders to opt for shares in companies which meet the cost of distributing their accounts to investors. Bad news.

THE CHEAPEST CHARGES

The sensible investors will put performance first, and then pick the PEP with the charging structure that best matches their own approach. There are so many possible variations that no one can claim with certainty to be the cheapest overall. The big four banks are all reasonably priced, however, with Barclays and Lloyds probably lowest, but they lack the investment flexibility of other schemes. Many of the stockbrokers' plans look relatively expensive, while the Fidelity-linked operators provide lots of useful trimmings which new investors especially may feel will be worth higher fees.

If you are serious about saving on charges, try to decide exactly how you will use your PEP over the next three years, then list each and every charge on your favourite plans. Only by such detailed work will you get a reasonably clear picture. A casual glance can be very deceptive. And then remember – the cheapest may not be the best.

4 Picking the PEP to Suit You

Never let anyone accuse the City of being slow to respond to innovation. In less than a year since the starting date, 200 or so PEPs have sprung to life, with something to suit almost every investment taste. Almost every plan offers a different twist in the way it works, or how it charges; and each one backs a different bunch of investments to make money for the PEP punters.

THE MEANING OF DISCRETION

Before you start trying to sort out which suits you best, you need to know what the PEP manager's idea of discretion is. There are two broad types of scheme – discretionary and non-discretionary. Discretionary management means that the manager takes the discretion away from the investor, that he has freedom to put what shares he wants into the fund, and take them out when he wants, telling the investor after he has done it, so long as he sticks to the broad rules outlined in the investment philosophy of the fund. Non-discretionary management means you do the choosing yourself.

The forces of the market and of bureaucracy have combined to ensure that most PEPs are discretionary, taking investment decisions away from the individual and putting them with the professional. It is yet another chip off the Chancellor's bold dream of millions of investors watching over the shares they have chosen. PEP rules make it more expensive to arrange do-it-yourself plans. Be consoled by the thought that it is probably much safer for the small, first-time investor to have

an experienced investment manager overseeing his money.
Sad, but true.

THE INVESTMENT SPREAD

It is a classic rule of investment that the wider the spread, the
smaller the risk. Put your money into two shares and you could
lose half if one goes wrong. Put it into twenty shares, then one
dud will not make too much difference. Equally, of course, it is
hard enough to pick one big winner, let alone two – and almost
impossible to pick twenty winners. So the wider the spread, the
lower the chance of making a real killing.
   Obviously this debate is very important to the PEP investor.
If you are a sophisticated shareholder, used to the way the
market rises and falls, you may be prepared to take a greater
risk and go for a PEP with a narrow spread of shares. If,
however, the PEP is your first venture into the stock market,
or if you have only played so far by backing the great
privatization new issue bonanza, then your views could be very
different.
   For newcomers, and for anyone looking to PEPs as a livelier
alternative to money in the bank, building society, or National
Savings, the clear rule is to go for a discretionary PEP, where
someone else provides the investment skills. Then the idea is to
pick the PEP with the widest possible spread of shares. That
way, you take the least risk. You may fare a little worse than
the stock market as a whole (the cost of dealing prevents the
average fund manager matching the average performance of
the market), but if the market continues to perform in the
exciting way it did between January 1975 and January 1987,
then you will have nothing to complain about. And you will
have left building society returns looking very mean.

THE PRINCIPAL PEP VARIATIONS

Three main patterns of discretionary PEP have emerged, each
following broadly the same style of operation. There are small

funds devoted entirely to unit trusts; funds which mix unit trusts and shares; and funds which invest wholly in shares. Many managers offer all three variations on these themes. Which should you choose?

UNIT TRUST PEPS

In theory, the safest and most conservative PEPs should be those invested entirely in unit trusts. As we have seen, you can put no more than £35 a month or a total of £420 into unit trusts or investment trusts in each PEP, unless you are also buying shares in that PEP, when the trust element can be up to a quarter of your total (a maximum of £600, or £50 a month).

Unit trusts offer an extra layer of management. The managers buy shares in companies they think will do well, and the price of the units rises or falls in relation to the prices of those shares. The size of each unit trust is determined by how much money investors put into it. Most unit trusts use that money to buy between 40 and 120 different shares, so they offer a very broad spread of risk.

Each unit trust will follow a clearly defined investment policy. Some are general trusts, taking a good mixture of shares in all sorts of companies, and aiming to score by generating a good total return, mixing capital gains with income. Some – usually with 'growth' in the trust title – will concentrate on capital gains, while others seek high income. Beyond that, there are trusts specializing in different areas of industry – high technology or gold, for example – or different geographical regions, such as the Far East, America, or France. Lowest risk of all are the general trusts.

The most cautious PEP investor, then, will concentrate on unit trusts, and on general unit trusts. That way there will be a very wide spread of risk.

There is an extra, and vital way of obtaining re-assurance when you back a unit trust; you can easily get an idea of just how good the managers are. The family finance pages of most newspapers regularly publish unit trust performance tables. How they have fared with the unit trusts they already run will give you an excellent – though not infallible – guide to how well-equipped they are to look after your PEP money. I discuss just how to pick the best manager in chapter five (page 30).

THE OVERSEAS ELEMENT

The more sophisticated investor, however, may use unit trusts as a means of spreading the risk around the world. Only UK-based shares are eligible for PEPs, but there is no restriction on buying UK-based unit trusts which invest wholly overseas. So, say, £600 in a Far East unit trust gives an extra touch of investment excitement not available through shares.

The Unit Trust Association will send you, free, general information on unit trusts. Write to them at Park House, 16, Finsbury Circus, London EC2M 7JP. Telephone: 01–638 3071.

INVESTMENT TRUSTS

Almost everything which applies to unit trusts in PEPs applies also to investment trusts. They offer a good spread of risk, and a way of buying into foreign markets. Investment trusts differ from unit trusts in that, while they buy a selection of shares on behalf of their investors, they have a fixed amount of capital themselves. Their shares are traded on the stock market, and supply and demand on the market governs their price – though that, of course, is influenced by the worth of the shares they hold themselves. Investment trusts can also borrow money to invest, and go for unquoted companies – things unit trusts cannot do. Borrowing money may yield a big return, if the managers use it to buy good shares. Unquoted companies are riskier than publicly traded ones, but get them right, and the rewards can be greater.

In fact, investment trusts are better value than unit trusts in many ways. Only rarely do their shares sell for more than the value of the investments they hold, so it is possible to buy them at a discount to the value of their holdings. That discount commonly varies between 10 per cent and 30 per cent. In recent years, there has been a flurry of takeover bids for investment trusts from people wishing to exploit that discount. They buy investment trust shares at below their value, then bid for the trust, and sell the shares the trust holds as a cheap way of raising money.

If you want investment trusts in your PEP, you need the advice of a stockbroker, preferably one of the stockbrokers specializing in investment trusts. The biggest and best are James Capel, Wood Mackenzie, and Alexanders Laing & Cruickshank, though other brokers give a competent trust service. Robin Boyle at regional brokers Stancliffe, at Warnford Court, 29, Throgmorton Street, London, EC2N 2AT (Telephone: 100 Freefone Stancliffe) offers a more personal service. Or you may prefer to pick one of the PEPs launched by investment trusts themselves. Alliance Investment Trust was one of the first in this field.

The Association of Investment Trust Companies pumps out a vast amount of literature, free of charge. Some of it is complicated, but there are genuinely useful leaflets as well. Write to them at Park House, 6th floor, 16, Finsbury Circus, London EC2M 7JJ (Telephone: 01–588 5347), for information on the way investment trusts work, and how to buy them.

UNITS AND EQUITIES

Next on the safety-first PEP list come those which combine holdings in unit trusts with ordinary shares – equities – chosen by the fund managers. In many cases, these amount to little more than unit trusts under a different guise, and with slightly more limited scope.

Take a manager like the Prudential Corporation. If offers a species of PEP which will put the first block of your money into its unit trusts, and then go on to spread the rest of your cash over its choice of twenty suitable shares, usually in sizeable companies.

Since the Pru will lump a lot of individual applications together to buy the shares at good rates, each investor coming in at a particular date will get the same selection of shares. Indeed, that selection may change only modestly over the months, according to the Pru's judgement of what is best. So investors end up with something like a unit trust – only instead of having 40 to 120 shares, which would be too expensive for the modest amount of money in a PEP, they have twenty shares. The spread is smaller, so the risk is slightly greater, but with top-flight, conservative managers like those at the Pru, there is little to fear. They go for the limited range, because they can watch a limited range like hawks – or that, anyway, is the theory.

Other PEP managers have similar schemes, buying and managing shares for their PEPs en bloc, but generally offering a smaller spread of shares than the Pru. Most give details of why they are buying what they choose.

SHARE-ONLY PEPS

It is a short step from PEPs which combine unit trust investments with shares to PEPs which leave out the unit trusts, and opt for shares alone. The shares normally come from a limited list of bigger companies, chosen by the managers, and bought in blocks to keep costs down. There is nothing wrong with this – the PEP will prosper or founder according to the ability of the managers. Clearly, most companies offering such schemes have great management experience, running unit trusts, with the record of their past transactions out where all can see it.

Once again, the number of shares in the PEP is worth watching – the smaller the number, the greater the risk. Once again, you are getting a mini unit trust, which ought to be pretty safe, backed by the skills of people who ought to understand what they are doing. Once again, it is not the same as investing yourself, with the thrill of picking your own winners and following your own investment ideas.

27

PEPS – DOING IT YOURSELF

If you do want to manage it yourself – and I am all in favour, so long as you understand the risk you are taking – there are some managers who will help. Because you are making the investment choices, you need worry less about the money-making abilities of your manager. Obviously, other things being equal, it makes sense to choose the longest-established, biggest management house, always making sure it is a member of the appropriate self-regulatory body.

Several big names offer a half-way house, where you can pick your own shares from a list they have approved. Perhaps the biggest choice of all is offered by Save & Prosper, the unit trust group. Its tally of eligible shares is now over 650, taking in most of the Alpha and Beta. It is concentrated on big names, but comes with reasonable charges across the board, and looks the most flexible of the major schemes.

Many other widely advertised schemes – like those linked to Fidelity and the clearing banks – allow you to choose shares from a more limited list which they have approved. In chapter eight (page 53) I look at the broad guide-lines you should use to pick shares for yourself.

If you want to go the whole hog, and plunge all of your cash into one or two shares, big names or small, you need a completely non-discretionary fund. For that, you almost certainly have to go to one of the more specialist, smaller managers like bankers Coutts, investment brokers Granville and Pointon York, or Birmingham stockbrokers Albert E. Sharp, though new PEP possibilities are appearing all of the time. The non-discretionary schemes are generally more expensive, but Sharp's charges are not too high. If you are determined to run your own PEP the way you see best, then cost should not deter you. If you can out-perform the average PEP manager, then spending a little more for that freedom will be well worthwhile.

Doing it yourself is much closer to the Chancellor's original idea of PEPs. But for the new investor, the risks are greater. For the experienced investor, of course, the PEP will be the ideal home for perhaps one or two pet shares on which to take a long-term view. Or perhaps the best place for the real gambling stocks.

5   How to Pick the Top PEP Managers

It sounds like a joke to say that PEP managers fall into three categories – good, bad, and indifferent. But it is true, and it will not be much fun if you pick a bad one. And if you have taken the trouble to dig into this book, you will clearly not feel content if you land yourself with an indifferent one. Nothing but the best should do.

There is no fool-proof way of spotting the best, no guarantee that you can pick one of the winners, simply because there are no guarantees in the share business. Once you step outside the cosy world of fixed-interest investment – either through banks, building societies, National Savings, or the various fixed-interest securities which are traded on the stock market – you are into the risk business.

THE RISK BUSINESS

The Government insists that unit trust advertising carries the warning that prices can fall as well as rise. It is a prudent note. Pick the best investment manager in the world, and he will not keep your cash intact if the whole stock market slumps. In theory, you might think he could sell your shares and put the money on deposit, earning interest until it is time to go back into shares. In practice, that never happens. It is asking too much of any adviser to spot the turn for you, and sell out at exactly the right moment. Many investment managers will not

30

want to, and some feel that you have bought their funds because you want the money to be in shares, not in cash.

So do not expect miracles. All you can expect is good, honest service from a good, honest manager, doing his best, and making more right decisions than wrong ones. Six winners out of ten is good enough, though in booming markets, you might do better.

SAFETY FIRST

Before you get down to worrying about performance, however, you really need to make sure than you pick a good, honest manager, one you can rely on to operate his business not just according to the rules, but in a fashion which really does put your interests uppermost. This is a topic I touched on earlier, when explaining who is allowed to run PEPs.

No matter what the rules, there cannot be total protection against dishonesty. But despite heavy publicity about those who go off the rails, it is relatively rare that investment managers in the UK do behave dishonestly. (Never, incidentally, deal with anyone who phones or writes to you from outside these shores). But there are some bad apples.

Happily, the Financial Services Act begins to bite in the autumn of 1987. It slings a safety net beneath the PEP investor. All being well, by the time you read this there will be a compensation fund which will give you the right to claim for losses of up to £30,000 in full where the manager has broken the rules, or gone broke through no fault of yours. In any dispute, there will be an ombudsman you can appeal to, without the expensive business of going to court.

Check to see that your PEP manager belongs to one of the bodies covered by the Financial Services Act, under the wing of the Securities & Investments Board (SIB). Before long, he will be operating illegally if he does not.

You can find the SIB at 3, Royal Exchange Buildings, London EC3V 3NL. Telephone: 01–283 2474. In practice, many PEP managers will be responsible first to FIMBRA, the Financial Intermediaries, Managers and Brokers Regulatory Association, 22, Great Tower Street, London EC3R 5AQ.

Telephone: 01–929 2711. Stockbrokers will be covered by The Securities Association, The Stock Exchange Building, London EC2N 1EQ. Telephone: 01–588 2355. Others may come under the Investment Management Regulatory Organization, 45, London Wall, London EC2M 5TE. Telephone: 01–256 7261.

Make sure that your PEP manager belongs to one of these organizations. The Financial Services Act is new. It is not perfect, but it should do a good job for most investors. It is possible that some PEP managers will be able to operate for a while without belonging to any of the above bodies. Avoid them.

THE APPROVED PECKING ORDER

Of course, official approval is no guarantee of best practice, and no indication of management ability. There is a kind of pecking order among the approved managers. They are not all equal.

At the risk of being unfair to some, the rule must be to choose from the biggest, longest-established names first, all else being equal. However, if you want a particular slant to your PEP which is not on offer from the big names, you have no choice but to look elsewhere.

I am a little sorry to say it, but for most PEP investors the soundest advice is to forget about smaller, perhaps local operators, and go to the big boys. Only use a smaller, local manager if you know him well, and can be absolutely sure about him. This advice will upset some thriving, vigorous investment managers who draw their strength from local communities. It is a hard judgement. Unfortunately, I have seen too many inexperienced investors entrust far too much money to advisers simply because they were handy, on the doorstep, and it was easy to pop in and talk.

That is a strength, and a weakness. It is far easier to be talked into something by a friendly face sitting opposite you than it is to fall prey to some come-on in a printed brochure which comes through the post. Local investment managers may be able to give individual attention, and to tailor their advice ideally to your needs. But they may not be quite so well in touch as big names in the big cities, with expensive research at their fingertips, and with well-established, clearly defined and carefully checked procedures to follow. Though there are spot-checks and accounting rules, the smaller, out-of-town man may be able to get away with a sloppier approach to your money than perhaps he should. A good local man is worth his weight in gold. But unless you are positive he is good, and can check him out independently, play safe and go for the bigger name.

UNIT TRUST MANAGERS

What then? For the average, uncertain PEP investor, the easiest schemes to assess are run by those who advertise their services as money managers. Many are already running unit trusts, with their wares regularly displayed in the financial pages. The Unit Trust Association (address on page 25) will supply information about the way they work. And the financial press publishes frequent performance tables.

The weekly *Investors Chronicle* (the best all-round magazine for investment), and monthly magazines like *Planned Savings, Money Observer, Money Management,* and *What Investment* carry long and sometimes comprehensive charts of performance.

From time to time there are surveys which attempt to assess individual management groups as a whole. These are the most valuable, but they take a lot of compiling. This is because most groups have a variety of trusts, each with different characteristics. Gold funds, for example, have done badly in recent years, no matter how good the manager, only to rush ahead in 1987. Many technology funds have lagged, while Japanese trusts have generally roared away on the back of the soaring Yen. Individual performances, influenced by special factors, distort the overall picture.

So concentrate on the mainstream funds, the general growth or income funds, and perhaps the recovery, or special situations trusts. These are the ones which will most closely resemble the investments which will be allowed under PEPs, and offer the truest all-round measure of a management group's ability.

The thing to watch for is good, consistent performance over a three-year period, or longer. Many tables show one, two, five and ten-year performance figures. Anyone who is consistently in the top half of managers listed over all of those periods is worth special attention.

If you want to bring a specialized unit trust into your PEP to gain exposure to a particular section – the Far East, say, or Europe – then you will want to see how each manager's comparable unit trusts have fared. Remember, past performance is no guarantee of the future. But it is about the best guide you will get.

BANKS AND INSURANCE COMPANIES

All the big banks have PEPs on offer, and their investment abilities can be gauged by the success of their unit trusts. They are solid, rather than spectacular. But they are keen to succeed in PEPs, and may do better with them.

Similarly, most insurance companies offering PEPs have unit trusts against which you can check performance. Some are fairly new to publicly promoted unit trusts, and have been keen to establish a good performance where all can see. It is sometimes possible to inflate the short-term performance of new trusts, making them look better than perhaps they will fare over the longer run. Bear that in mind, and weight your assessment slightly in favour of the longer-established funds.

STOCKBROKERS

Assessing the ability of stockbrokers is much trickier. Some run unit trusts, and most have proved fairly good at it. Tread warily, however, if the PEP is the broker's first stab at a widely promoted investment fund. Brokers may do well, but you may find that their main business of buying and selling shares absorbs most of their efforts. The PEP may be a side-show to keep a few clients happy, or simply be there because they think they should show the flag. There is no substitute for personal recommendation when choosing stockbrokers, and unless you can rely on that, opt for a PEP whose potential you can measure by reference to a unit trust.

INVESTMENT MANAGERS

Similar thoughts apply to investment managers. If there is no established publicly promoted vehicle to help you rate their investment skills, go elsewhere, unless you are sure they are the ones for you.

BUILDING SOCIETIES

Building societies are the most intriguing players to come into PEPs. Many will be there simply as a matter of self-defence, seeking to avoid losing deposits to people attracted by possible higher returns outside building society accounts. They have no established investment skills themselves. They will want to do well, but their culture is risk-averse, and it is hard for old dogs to learn new tricks. Their attractions will depend largely on their ready accessibility, and just who they hire to manage their PEPs. The Abbey National, for example, has stuck its name on a scheme which is essentially the Fidelity plan with a few knobs on. Investment performance will depend on how good Fidelity is. Not bad at all, is the answer.

The Bradford & Bingley has gone for stockbrokers James Capel as managers. Their record is not widely trumpeted, but they are one of the most powerful broking firms in the City. They should be good news.

If some of the above advice appears harsh, so be it. I hope this book will help the experienced investor but, inevitably, it must be concerned most with the relatively new share buyer; or perhaps the investor who is looking at the stock market for the first time, and sees PEPs as the simple way in.

In twenty-five years as a financial journalist, I have seen the worries and confusion which so many investors experience. And I have seen how easily they are led astray, or become hopelessly muddled by the fine print. It puts many off the investment world for life. That is sad.

So, above all, my judgements are aimed at protecting PEP investors. Complete assurance is impossible. But it is vital that investment beginners learn the way one step at a time, and tread as carefully as possible. Once again, then, I am sorry if my advice is hard on some investment managers. But for most readers of this book, I am certain, safety first is what counts at all costs.

6   Who's Who in PEPs

It is inviting trouble to attempt to list the PEP managers, to say who is biggest, who is best, and who should be shown the door. That is sure to upset all but those who top the list. And since there are PEP managers popping up with new schemes almost every day, no such tally could hope to be complete.

Ducking the issue, however, would be to fail in a book of this sort. In the end, who you choose is up to you, and your choice will be influenced by your own particular needs. But it makes sense to consider some of the most widely promoted plans, and what they offer. Some of the individual comments may offer a useful clue to assessing the value of other plans which are not discussed in detail.

THE PRUDENTIAL

Most respected of the insurance giants, the Prudential has investment strength in depth. The Pru can make things happen. The best-known example of the Pru making things happen occurred when the company led other big investors to force a change of top management at the Rank Organisation, the cinemas and copying machines giant. That has proved a great success. And there are many other public companies where the Pru's muscle has helped to shape events.

The Pru is a privileged investor. New ideas are often quietly shown to the Pru first, to see if they are worth pushing through. And though the Pru has its own analysts, stockbrokers often put the Pru at the head of the list when they come up with a good investment idea.

All of this means the Pru ought to do a little better than the average investment manager. And it does. Since the Pru began to promote its *Holborn unit trusts* widely, it has done well. The skills behind the Pru's PEPs ought to pay off.

The Prudential *Uni Plan* allows an investment of up to £420 into any of the Pru's Holborn unit trusts.

The *Multi Plan* allows monthly payments into a combination of Holborn unit trusts and shares.

The *Equi Plan* allows a lump sum investment into a mixture of Holborn unit trusts and shares.

Investors can choose which trust they want in the unit-only plan, but investment choices in the other two are made by the Pru. There will be a spread of up to twenty shares, chosen largely from the top 100 companies, with an emphasis on total return (income and capital gains together). The managers will send out quarterly reports.

No charges will be levied until the end of the second year, so that investors get the benefit of capital growth on the whole of their investment. Dealing charges are a modest 0·2 per cent.

Disadvantages: The managers are not anxious to encourage investors to attend meetings of the companies in which they hold shares because of the cost of organising it. There is a charge of 10 per cent of the sum invested for attending meetings.

Details: Prudential Portfolio Managers Ltd, PEP Division, Freepost, Ilford, Essex IG1 1BR. Free telephone line: 0800 345 345.

SAVE & PROSPER

One of the biggest names in unit trusts, established in 1934, Save & Prosper has gone for PEPs with enthusiasm. After an indifferent spell, management skills have been sharpened, and indifferent spell, management skills have been sharpened, and though Save & Prosper is rarely among the top performers, it has a reliable reputation. It owns stockbrokers Montagu Loebl Stanley, and is steadily expanding services to private investors.

One PEP allows a choice of any of the twenty-eight Save & Prosper unit trusts, or the *Masterfund*, an actively managed fund which switches between the group's various unit trusts, giving an attractive spread of world markets and different areas of specialization.

The *Managed Portfolio* takes a lump sum of £500 or more, or monthly payments, and puts it into a portfolio of about ten well-known companies selected by the managers. The cash is invested in blocks of £200. There are half-yearly statements showing plan details, and six-monthly newsletters.

The *Dealing Service* is one of the most attractive of all do-it-yourself PEP opportunities. On a minimum investment of £500, you can pick your own shares out of an impressive list of more than 650 leading companies. Save & Prosper will try to lump purchases together to pass on savings in dealing costs.

The initial charges are deducted from lump sums and regular subscriptions, so it is best for investors to add them to the sum they send in, to get the full amount of cash into the PEP. For example, a lump sum investment of £2,400 requires a cheque for £2,442.12 to cover initial costs. This method makes sense in several other plans, too. There is an attractive option of depositing cash in the *Robert Fleming High Interest Bank Account* at 1 per cent less than the Fleming rate. This pays interest related to money market rates, comfortably above those on normal bank accounts. It is ideal for anyone wishing to earn tax-free interest with safety by staying in cash in a PEP until the last minute for switching into shares.

Disadvantages: Save & Prosper's investment record is sound, but not the most dynamic. Once again, attendance at company meetings is discouraged with a charge of £25 a meeting.

Details: Save & Prosper Equity Plan Managers Ltd, 1, Finsbury Avenue, London EC2M 2QY. Telephone: 01–588 1717. Telephone free for customer services on: Moneyline 0800 282 101.

LLOYDS BANK

All the big four banks are absolutely safe with regard to PEPs. Lloyds has one of the best-value schemes for those who want a do-it-yourself element. As unit trust managers, Lloyds have done reasonably well over the medium-term, and especially well in *Smaller Companies and Recovery*, with a very successful *Extra Income* fund. As with all of the big banks, you do not need to be a customer of the bank to buy the PEP, and details are available at all bank branches.

Lloyds Bank Managed PEP aims at combining growth with low risks. It takes monthly subscriptions or a lump sum, and mixes the bank's unit trusts with up to four shares from a list of thirty chosen by the bank.

There is also a *Choice PEP* allowing customers to select from a list of unit trusts of thirty approved shares. Cash can be held in a high-interest cheque account. There is an annual valuation and statement, and clients are sent advice notes after each deal.

The charge for attending meetings is only £5.

Details: Lloyds Bank plc, Elizabeth House, 9–11, Bush Lane, London EC4P 4LN. Telephone: 01–623 1288. Or bank branches, or Lloyds Bank plc, Personal Equity Plan Centre, FREEPOST, Haywards Heath, West Sussex RH16 3ZA.

BARCLAYS BANK

Barclays is making a big effort to push PEPs, and the all-round package looks sound and attractive. There is a *Barclayshare Managed Scheme*, a one-stock *Barclayshare* for experienced investors, and a unit-trust-only scheme. As trust managers, Barclays' performance is in the middle of the range, but the bank's early showing on PEP share selections has been good in a rising market.

The Barclayshare scheme picks four shares, including an investment trust to give an extra spread of risk. Investors can specify whether they are seeking income, capital gains, or balanced growth. They are sent a contract note for each purchase detailing costs, and giving a brief explanation of the reasons for choosing the share – a very welcome idea.

The unit-trust-only scheme goes into *Barclays Unicorn General*, a sensible middle-of-the-road trust.

There is no charge for attending company meetings.

Details: Barclayshare Centre, Box 205, Watford WD1 1BP. Telephone: 0923 46333. Or bank branches.

MIDLAND BANK

The Midland has a steady performance as a unit trust manager. The PEP lacks the flair of the Barclays scheme. The *Managed Plan* puts up to £420 a year into the Midland's *Unit Trust Income Fund*, with the rest in major UK shares.

There is an attendance charge of £10 for company meetings.

Details: Midland Bank Trust Company, Courtwood House, Silver Street Head, Sheffield S1 3RD. Telephone 0742 529077. Or bank branches.

NATIONAL WESTMINSTER BANK

Another middle-of-the-road performer, National Westminster Bank is offering a *Managed Scheme*, a unit trust scheme called *Spreadplan*, and a *Share Plan*.

The Managed Scheme chooses three big companies from a list of about thirty, while the Share Plan allows the customer to choose from an approved list. The unit trust scheme picks the trust of the manager's choice, and started with County Income & Growth.

If you want full voting and attendance rights, there is a charge of £100 a year, but no charge for merely attending meetings.

Details: NATWEST PEP Office, 11, Old Broad Street, London EC2N 1BB. Or bank branches.

FIDELITY

Fidelity has promoted PEPs with real commitment, supported by a sophisticated computer back-up, and a reputation for lively unit trust management which makes it among the most consistent top performers of the 1980s.

An investor services team is on tap, seven days a week, offering individual advice on how best to set up your PEP. Investors get a 'welcome pack' detailing their portfolio, and letters explaining any portfolio change. Fidelity is keen on seminars to meet investors around the country, and issues a regular newsletter on PEPs. Charges are on the high side, depending on how they are calculated, but the schemes are highly recommended to investors who want extra attention.

The *Share Plan* will invest 75–80 per cent of the cash in between five and eight top shares and growth companies picked by the managers, with up to 25 per cent in the *Fidelity Growth & Income* unit trust.

The unit trust PEP will go into the trust of the manager's choice, initially Fidelity Growth & Income.

There is a charge of £20 a year for each company for attending meetings.

Details: Fidelity, River Walk, Tonbridge, Kent TN9 1DY. Telephone: 0800 414161 free of charge.

M & G

Another top unit trust group, with a splendid reputation for sound long-term performance, M & G has been slow taking up the PEP challenge. Whatever M & G does, however, will be done with care and a real responsibility to clients. As we go to print, there is no managed PEP, but there should be one in the second half of 1987.

The M & G unit trust plan gives a choice from virtually any of the group unit trusts.

Details: M & G House, Victoria Road, Chelmsford CM1. Telephone: 0245 266266. Or Advisory Services Department, Telephone: 01-626 4588.

MIM BRITANNIA

MIM Britannia is the relatively recent combination of the large Britannia group of unit trusts, which has a distinctly patchy performance, with the smaller and brighter MIM group. MIM has effectively taken over, and may boost performance.

There is a unit trust scheme with a choice of five MIM Britannia trusts, a *Blue Chip Portfolio*, and a *Special Situations Portfolio*.

The Blue Chip is 25 per cent invested in house unit trusts, with the rest in top-quality shares. Special Situations is an attractive idea for the slightly more adventurous investor, with a quarter of the fund in house unit trusts, and the rest in three of the kind of shares which might see extra action, through bids or other developments.

There is a charge of £35 a year for attending meetings.

Details: MIM Britannia, 74–78, Finsbury Pavement, London EC2A 1JD. Telephone: 01-588 2777.

ABBEY NATIONAL BUILDING SOCIETY

One of the biggest building societies, the Abbey National has adopted the *Fidelity PEP* scheme, which is eminently suited to those who may be new to share investment.

Details: Abbey National Building Society, Freepost, Bletchley, Milton Keynes MK1 1QW. Telephone: Dial 100 and ask for Freefone Adviceline PEP. Or any Abbey National branch.

BRADFORD & BINGLEY BUILDING SOCIETY

Another substantial and solid building society, the Bradford & Bingley has teamed up with top stockbrokers James Capel for the *Market Master*. Invested in up to ten shares and investment trusts, the plan will rely on Capel's good reputation, which is especially strong in investment trusts.

Details: Bradford & Bingley PEPs, PO Box 50, Bingley, Yorks.

KLEINWORT GRIEVESON

Top merchant bankers Kleinwort Benson bought brokers Grieveson Grant ahead of the Big Bang. Grieveson's strong image as a major private client broker was marred in the spring of 1987 when it withdrew a low-cost, no-frills dealing service because it could not keep up with the volume of business.

There is a unit trust PEP using *Barrington General Fund*, one of the old Grieveson-managed trusts which had a good name. The *Managed Equity Plan* combines a unit trust, and up to six growth shares.

The fee for attending meetings is £40 a plan each year.

Details: Kleinwort Grieveson & Co., PO Box 191, 10, Fenchurch Street, London EC3M 3LB. Telephone: 01-623 8000.

ALBERT E. SHARP

Birmingham stockbroker Albert E. Sharp is well respected, and offers an attractive deal for those wishing to choose their own shares.

Details: Albert E. Sharp, Edmund House, 12, Newhall Street, Birmingham B3 3ER. Telephone: 021 236 5801.

FRAMLINGTON

A medium-sized unit trust group which grew out of a stock-broker, Framlington is highly rated. It has chosen to create a unit trust especially for the PEP, managed by John Cornes, who has a good reputation. He will aim for capital growth from top UK shares.

Details: Framlington PEP 87, 3, London Wall Buildings, London EC2M 5NQ. Telephone: 01–628 5181.

HOARE GOVETT

One of the biggest and most reputable stockbrokers, Hoare Govett has a private client department which takes trouble to look after smaller investors. The Hoare PEP portfolio is managed by the eminently sensible Alan Izzard, who will be looking for conservative capital growth with reasonable charges.

There is a fee of £30 for attending each meeting.

Details: Andrew Townend, PEP Department, Hoare Govett Financial Services Ltd, Heron House, 319–325, High Holborn, London WC1V 7PB. Telephone:.01–404 0344.

SMITH & WILLIAMSON

A medium-sized, specialist financial services group, Smith & Williamson offer a sophisticated PEP to appeal to the experienced investor. There are only four subscription dates each year, and the maximum £2,400 must be invested.

Details: Smith & Williamson Securities, No. 1, Riding House Street, London W1A 3AS. Telephone: 01-637 5377.

COMMERCIAL UNION

Making an aggressive effort to win a reputation in fund management, the once-troubled insurance giant is pushing the CU Personal Equity plan hard. Managed by stockbrokers Ashton Tod McLaren, now owned by CU, the PEP mixes CU's unit trusts with blue chip shares. Reasonable charges.

Details: Commercial Union Assurance, PO Box 420, St Helens, Undershaft, London EC3 3DQ. Telephone: 01–283 7500.

45

7 Running Your Own PEP

Expert managers galore are on tap, eager for the opportunity to get their hands on your PEP cash, and to show you what they can do with it. That will not suit everybody. For many investors, the pick-'em yourself approach will be the one they want. That has considerable attractions, more obviously perhaps for the experienced investor than for the beginner. But if making a killing on privatization issues has lured you into the share market for the first time, and you fancy carrying on making the decisions for yourself, then PEPs offer the ideal way of learning.

Time and again, it is worth emphasizing that the share market is riskier than you think. Just when you reckon you have got the hang of it, and feel you need worry less about your investments, it will turn round and hit you. The moment you feel secure is the moment you have lost control. So do not think of running your own PEP unless you are prepared to keep a close eye on it, and are using money you can afford to lose.

PEP BEGINNERS PLEASE

That said, PEPs are pretty good for investment beginners. Because you must have a manager, there is always a professional in the background to guide you on the actual mechanics of buying and selling. There is no need to flog around looking for someone to do it for you, and to worry whether you are using the right chap and getting the best deal. The PEP forces you to make that choice before you start, when you choose which company's PEP best suits you. And, as we have seen, most of the managers in the PEP game are sound, solid citizens who will see things are done properly.

It makes sense, too, to try a PEP as your first do-it-yourself venture into shares because it forces you to limit the cash you are putting up. For some people, £2,400 will be a major investment, and they will not be able to afford the full load. Whatever your circumstances, a maximum of £2,400 is not a bad limit for learning purposes. It is big enough to bring worthwhile rewards if you get it right, and yet modest enough not to mean financial disaster if you get it wrong.

All too often I see the grim consequences for inexperienced investors who dabble unwisely – especially in commodity-linked schemes – and get carried away by their own over-enthusiasm, or sucked in by unscrupulous salesmen. They start small, and end up pumping in more and more money to retrieve their first mistake, and then lose much more than they can afford. That cannot happen with PEPs.

Freedom from the bother of accounting to the Inland Revenue is also a useful bonus for beginners, and the absence of taxes makes it all the tastier. If you pick the right PEP, of course, your dealing charges are more modest than they would be if you were investing in the normal way. So if you do feel like dabbling in shares, backing your own judgement, do not let anyone put you off a PEP. It can be a very good way in – though, remember, you cannot put new issues directly into it.

THE BASIC FRAMEWORK

If you are going to manage your own PEP, you need to start with a basic investment framework in mind. If you have got this far into the book, you will be familiar with the background, and the sort of simple decisions facing you – nothing too tricky, apart, of course, from the formula for picking winners. That comes in a later chapter.

HOW LONG

First you need to decide how long you are going to play the game. Because you need to hold for at least one calendar year to qualify for tax relief, you should not approach a PEP with too short a period in mind. Plan to keep the whole portfolio operating indefinitely; assume you will enjoy investment, and that you will be able to do well enough to keep your interest alive. In any event, you should not start with the notion of throwing in your hand, in normal circumstances, in less than three years. It will take that long for the tax advantages of PEPs to make a real impact, and it would be rash to expect your shares to do anything too exciting within that period – though they might. Ideally, you ought to assume your PEP experiment will run at least five years.

That is not to say that every share you buy need be bought on a five-year view, nor that you need hold any share for any minimum period. You can buy one day, and sell the next, if you are convinced there is a good reason for doing so. Obviously, such a swift change of mind would be unusual, and would tend to happen only when you had made a mistake and needed to retrieve the situation quickly. But so long as you keep within the limits of your PEP, you can buy and sell as often as you like. Equally obviously, too much buying and selling is expensive, and the cost of dealing will cancel out any gains you make. Never, though, allow considerations of dealing cost to deter you from selling – taking a profit or cutting a loss – if there is a good investment case for change. On page 58 I discuss the sensible way to approach buying and selling decisions.

INCOME – OR CAPITAL GAIN?

Your time-frame in place, the next decision is whether you are going to pick shares for income or for capital gain. Your own temperament and circumstances will play a part in this, and you should not be influenced too much by the tax structure of your PEP. Simply because Capital Gains Tax exemption limits are so high (you can realize profits of £6,600 before paying gains tax in 1987–88), the gains tax exemption of PEPs is not worth worrying about in normal circumstances except over the very long-term. The merit of tax-free investment income will begin to build up from year two onwards, and will be a major attraction for more conservative investors, and for those approaching retirement.

In the early years of the portfolio it makes sense, however, to place the greatest emphasis on capital growth, or on shares with the prospect of rising income, which will often amount to much the same thing. Companies which raise their dividends and give investors an increasing income are, by and large, the companies with good growth prospects and rising profits – the very companies which also attract investors looking for capital growth.

Strip away the mysteries and mumbo-jumbo of investment, and the big boys – insurance companies, pension funds and such – are buying shares for a future stream of higher income so that they can meet their pay-out commitments to policyholders and pensioners. So rising company profits and the increasing income they generate are at the very root of investment.

If you can generate strong capital gains in your PEP, the increase in income will follow. It will come either from rising dividends from the shares you have bought, or because you can take your gains and switch your increased capital to shares with a higher return. That way, you get a double income boost, putting more capital than you had at the start into shares which are giving a greater return than those you had at the start.

Clearly this kind of approach can be applied not just to PEPs where you pick your own shares, but also to unit trust PEPs where you can switch from one trust to another – though you will often find that, taking income and capital growth together, the total returns on high income unit trusts mean they are every bit as good for increasing capital as the growth trusts.

TOTAL RETURN

Indeed, for many investors it makes sense to worry less about choosing capital gains or income, and simply settling for the

49

best total return. Since gains and income are tax-free in PEPs, all that really matters is what happens to your lump sum. So long as that goes up, who cares what makes it rise?

RISKS AND REWARDS

That said, it is important to keep one of the fundamental rules of the money world to the fore – the greater the risk, the greater the reward. If you buy a share which offers a higher return than the market average, there will be a reason for it.

Either the capital growth prospects of that share will be correspondingly less attractive, or there may be a chance that the dividend payment which that high yield is derived from may be reduced in the future, or – hip-hooray! – you have spotted an undervalued share which will rise when the rest of the market spots it. But do not count on it. More often than not, an above-average yield will be there for a reason. It is just that you have not discovered that reason yet.

Always remember, the dividend yields you see in the newspapers and in most tip sheets or comments from stockbrokers, are based on the last year's dividend, unless there is a note explaining otherwise. Last year's dividend is not necessarily the same as this year's. Dividends fall as well as rise. So tread carefully if you are attracted by a yield which is out of line.

Different types of companies do have different yields. These reflect the market's view of prospects for each sector. Stores, for example, tend to have lower yields than oil shares these days. That reflects the sensible opinion that the business outlook for store profits is more buoyant and assured than that for companies dependent on a sharply fluctuating price of oil.

It is not just shares with a higher yield which carry higher-than-average risks, however. Some shares with very low yields may also be high-risk investments, for a different reason. They may have a low yield because their dividend has been cut and the company is in trouble. Or because the stock market has decided to accept a low yield for the moment because the chances of capital growth are exceptionally good. That is fine, so long as that growth does come through. But if the company should falter, a very highly rated share can plummet as it falls from favour. So watch out. An exceptionally low yield may not carry quite the risk an exceptionally high one does. But it can have drawbacks. Unless you are confident of what you are doing, stick to shares with yields around the average while you learn the ropes.

AVERAGE YIELDS

You can find sector averages each day in the *Financial Times*, where there is a table of all of the main stock market indices – the measures of share price performance. What you want is the section headed 'FT-Actuaries Indices'. Under 'Equity Groups & Sub-Sections' you will find what you need, with dividend yields in the column marked 'Gross Div. Yield pc'. Any shares which give a return which differs by more than two points from the average are doing that for a special reason, good or bad. Investigate before buying. In chapter nine, on investment basics, I explain what some of the other columns in the Indices list mean.

SPREADING THE RISK

There is more, though, to stock market risk than just the individual shares you choose. You must also decide how many shares you should have in your PEP. Earlier, we touched on the spread of investments, and the notion that the more shares you buy, the safer your money. One loser in ten will not be so costly as one loser in two, and the other nine ought to be able to make up for it. The opposite applies, of course. One winner in ten will not be nearly as rewarding as if you had split your cash between just two shares, and one of them turned out to be a winner.

The standard City approach is to suggest that the wider the spread, the better for the new investor. The emphasis is on safety first. Quite right it is, too, for many people. But it should not be regarded as an inviolable rule.

So long as you understand that the fewer the shares in your PEP, the greater the risk, there is no reason why you should not bang your whole £2,400 on one flyer. The sophisticated investor may well play that way – but his £2,400 will only be a small part of a bigger portfolio, with shares outside PEP to spread his risk. If exemption from Capital Gains Tax is going to mean anything to PEP investors in the first year or two, they need to gamble to make the kind of profits which would have been heavily taxed outside it. The serious and experienced investor might well decide a PEP is the obvious home for the riskiest share in his list, the one that could quadruple in a year – some do, believe me – or go bust.

If you are a first-timer and you want to play the high-risk way, go ahead, so long as you do it with your eyes wide open. More people want to treat shares as a wild gamble than the City would like to admit. Good luck.

If you want to walk a steadier line, however, spread your risk. Some managed schemes give quite a wide spread – up to twenty shares. That is too much for the individual investor. The cost of dealing is too high. It seems sensible not to deal in units of less than £500 a share, which means that four shares is about right for a do-it-yourself PEP policy.

In many ways, I feel inclined to suggest that even four is too many, and that three or even two would be better. Then, if you get it right, the gain is well worth having. Where it is possible to double the input with two PEPs and a total investment of £4,800, I would not choose more than six shares altogether. Spotting one winner is hard enough. Picking six is too much to ask.

Once again, though, this will be a matter for individual judgement. Perhaps I have been around the market too long, and have a personal bias towards too adventurous an investment policy for everyone's taste. In the end, you have to decide for yourself. If you are inclined to pick shares yourself in a PEP, go ahead. That way you will learn much more about the exciting business of investment.

8 How to Spot a Winning Share

You are geared up, ready to go. You know how PEPs work, how to choose the managers, whether you should spread the risk, and you have decided to pick the shares yourself. You are poised to go forth and make a killing in the share jungle.

Now comes the really difficult part – picking the shares themselves. Difficult? It should be easy, surely? Every day, the City pages have lists full of prices which have gone up, dozens and dozens of them on some days. Great fun. But when it comes down to actually putting your money up, choosing which shares to buy for real, it can be frightening. That is when you notice that there are many days when lots of shares do not move at all. And many days when dozens of shares go down, sometimes quite sharply.

And though you recognize names like Marks & Spencer, ICI, British Telecom, and British Gas, what does a company like BTR do? Or BOC? Or Rolls-Royce? Is that the one which makes the cars? (It is not. Vickers owns the Rolls-Royce car business. Rolls-Royce makes the aero engines).

The investment business is a jungle, full of traps for the unwary. It can be confusing, intimidating, and totally off-putting. But it can also be enormous fun, and highly profitable. It helps to know the rules, to understand how investment decisions are made by the big players. But you can get by with just common-sense and good fortune.

STICK TO WHAT YOU KNOW

The simplest common-sense rule is to stick to what you know.

There is an awful lot of jargon in the City, massively compli-cated ways of doing massively complicated things. Half of the people who work in the City do not understand much of what is going on much of the time. Do not be deceived by appear-ances, or by a smooth line in chat. Never hesistate to ask about things you do not understand. If you cannot understand the explanation, walk away. Perhaps the person who is explaining it to you does not understand it too well, either. Whatever the case, if you cannot follow it, it is not for you. There are plenty of other opportunities.

WHERE TO FIND OUT

There is an enormous amount of valuable information on offer, free of charge, in and about the City. First point of call should be the Stock Exchange. The trading floor may no longer be buzzing in the Stock Exchange Tower, but the Stock Exchange is thriving on electronic communication systems which tie in everyone around the City and many who work miles outside. The Stock Exchange Council does a good job trying to help investors understand how it all works, and supplies excellent brochures – most of them free – on a variety of investment topics, excluding share tips. Write to The Stock Exchange, London EC2N 1HP, for a list of their publications, and find time to read them.

If your PEP manager is a stockbroker, try to sound him out for ideas. He may be reluctant to give them to you. Brokers have become more cost-conscious, charging for their time. A small investor may well get a more sympathetic hearing from a local broker in the provinces than a big London name. It is always worth asking your broker what he thinks, and for copies of reports on companies which his research department are putting out to clients.

The financial press is invaluable and inexpensive. The *Financial Times* provides the most comprehensive investor service of all daily newspapers, listing thousands of share prices and their movements, plus the longest daily list of unit trust prices, and reports on a string of other markets. The Lex column on the back page is still the most influential column in the share market, but the *FT* does relatively little share-tipping.

The *Daily Mail* is seen by many as the ideal companion for the *FT*. Space for City news in the *Mail* is limited, but there is good, pointed coverage of the essentials, plus sharp comment and the kind of gossip and rumour which so often indicates what is really going on. The *Mail* stock market report is one of the best in the business, and all investors should pay special attention to the market reports.

Although there are breaks from time to time, I contribute a fairly regular share-tipping column to the *Mail* with special emphasis on when to sell – a service omitted by many tipping columns, which return most readily to their successes, forget the losers, and to give little guidance on selling.

The financial columns vary in quality, but carry an enormous amount of ideas and information. Financial journalists move around frequently, however. Find one who makes sense to you, and follow him. Be a little wary of columns which are not signed with the individual author's name. Their quality can change sharply when one contributor moves on and another takes over, unannounced, under the same name.

Financial journalists do get things wrong sometimes, of course. Who doesn't? But financial journalists have no particular product to sell, other than their newspaper. That gives them the virtue of being independent observers at a time when the scene is full of salesmen masquerading as advisers. This is not to dismiss salesmen completely. Many have first-class products, and give a fine service. Some do not.

Highly recommended each week is the *Investors Chronicle*. Pay special attention to the summarized company reports in the back. They give invaluable data in handy form. *Financial Weekly* carries summaries of reports on different companies by stockbrokers. Among the monthly magazines, *Money Observer* is easily the most useful, though *What Investment* has a chatty style.

Tip sheets should not be ignored. The best of them are well-researched, and although no one can keep up with all of the ideas they offer, they are often good value. The snag is that – as with all tips – they can send a lot of people rushing for the same shares at once, forcing prices up in a flurry. *Fleet Street Letter*, *Penny Share Guide*, and *Penny Share Focus* are all sensible.

Beware, though, of newsletters which come free of charge from investment houses based outside this country. Most mix moderate comment on big stocks with glowing reports of small dubious companies whose shares are being pushed heavily by the operators behind the tip sheet. Almost invariably, you will receive telephone calls trying to pressure you into buying such shares. Almost invariably, the shares are vastly over-priced duds, and you could well lose *all* of your investment. Almost invariably, they will not be allowed by the Inland Revenue for inclusion in a PEP portfolio. Please, please, *please* do not buy shares from strangers over the phone. Most of them simply want to steal your money. Believe me, I know. I have dealt with hundreds of their victims.

When you spot a share which interests you, it may be possible to unearth the facts and figures about the company at your library. Most large libraries stock Extel cards, which summarise the financial history of the company. The cards also give names of the directors, their share stakes, and the registered office of the company. If you write to the Company Secretary at that address, most firms will send you their report and accounts. Some include a brochure giving a fuller explanation of just what the company does.

You can also get an outline of the company's history from the *Stock Exchange Official Yearbook*, which is in many libraries. That also carries the company's registered address.

Never hesitate to write to any company which appeals to you. Most are eager to respond. Watch, too, for advertisements in the financial press reporting profits.

USING YOUR EYES

Keep an eye open wherever you go. There are investment tips all around. Who is running the Marks & Spencer mail order catalogue? Who is this Blue Arrow company advertising employment agencies on TV? What will happen to housebuilders and their profits when mortgage rates fall? Did your local Curry's electrical shop suddenly come to life? Was it after Dixons had taken it over? Did that make Dixons' shares worth buying? Stock market killings have been made on elementary questions like that. Keep awake.

9 Is It Cheap? – The Investment Basics

Once you have spotted a share which sounds interesting, you have taken the first step towards successful investment. Then you have to try to decide whether the shares are worth buying. After all, you may just have chanced on one good part of the business in a struggling company. Or perhaps everyone in the City knew ages ago about what you have just discovered, and the shares have shot up as a result.

Deciding what makes a share cheap or dear is the art of investment. And there is no absolute answer. Whenever you buy a share, someone is selling. They may be selling because they need the money for something else. But they may be selling because they think the share is too dear. For every buyer, there has to be a seller. Both cannot be right.

INSIDERS AND ANTICIPATION

Share prices rise when more people want to buy than want to sell. On the surface, it is as simple as that. But what makes more buy than sell is really anticipation. That is what stock market prices are all about. Some say the stock market looks six months ahead. And sometimes it does. At other times, you will find it is looking two years ahead, or maybe just two weeks. What happened yesterday is of relatively little value in moving share prices. What happens today could be – if it is unexpected – but what counts most is what might happen next – and whether everybody else knows about it.

So by the time you discover the name of the firm supplying

some promising new product to a High Street store chain, it might be very stale news indeed. It probably first began to boost the share price soon after the directors began talking to the store group, and bought a share or two themselves (whatever the rules about insider trading, it happens all of the time, and it always will), and then the shares moved up a little more when others in the trade heard a whisper that talks had started.

Then a few more privileged people heard as the talks continued. And the company's stockbrokers began to get a glimmer, and tucked a few shares away, just in case. By the time the contract was signed, the brokers had probably been tipped the wink. So they joined the directors and a few of their chums in buying shares. The brokers bought quite a lot, in order to have some to sell when they started telling their most privileged clients to buy. Once the word went out to those privileged clients, they mentioned it to their friends, who bought. The company's banking advisers knew by then, of course. Some of them bought, and so did the investment funds advised by the bank.

The time came then to tell the investing public. The public relations advisers were called in to help write the statement. A few more shares were bought. Word went round that a big announcement was coming, and other brokers began to ask what was up. They heard the whispers, so they bought a few. The announcement of the contract was sent to the Stock Exchange. The first nimble buyers did quite well. Next day, it was in the financial press, and small shareholders bought some. When the goods actually got into the shops, there was a press conference for the trade. A few people saw the potential and bought shares. By the time you spotted the goods in the shops, and found out who made them, no one in the City needed telling what was up.

By then, perhaps, the word was getting round that the cost of setting up production lines for the new contract would eat into profits this year. And there had been problems with another major order, so profits might take a tumble. The chaps in the know had already started selling. This year would not be so good after all. That was why you found it easy to buy, and why the shares began to drift down.

A grossly exaggerated tale? Perhaps. But it is not too far off the truth. Anticipation is the name of the game in the City. Some of it comes down to intelligent assessment of what might happen. Much of it comes down to using whatever information you can get before the next chap. The City thrives on information, masses of it from all manner of places. And the small investor often stands last in line to hear it.

Do not expect to beat the so-called experts. The system is biased in their favour. The company news you see in the newspapers each day is almost invariably known in the City the day before, and share prices respond then. They only move if the news is not what had been expected. That is why shares can tumble on the announcement of a good rise in profits – because the City was expecting not just good, but phenomenal. And why sometimes shares rise on news of a thumping great loss: it may not have been as great as anticipated. The small investor cannot beat that system.

What the small investor can do, however, is use a measure of common-sense which sometimes eludes the City slickers, where from time to time they fail to see the wood for the trees. To apply that common-sense properly, it is best to be familiar with the simple framework of the figures which influence share prices.

DIVIDEND YIELDS

Dividend yields cropped up in an earlier chapter, where we discussed whether you should go for capital growth or income in your PEP. The dividend yield is the return you get from your investment through the dividend cheque the company sends out each year. Dividends usually rise or fall as profits rise or fall, and most companies pay twice a year – the interim, or half-year dividend – and the final, when profits for the whole year are known. Usually, the final dividend is greater than the interim.

The yield shows how much dividend you can expect from every £100 invested in the shares of each company. You do not really need to know how to calculate the yield, because it is widely reported in newspaper price tables. Assuming the amount of the dividend paid by the company is unchanged, the yield falls as share prices rise (because it costs you more to buy the right to the same fixed amount of dividend), and rises as the share price falls. If the company raises the dividend, then the yield automatically rises, just as it falls if the dividend is reduced.

Similar types of companies tend to be rated on similar yields. Companies the market thinks have good capital growth prospects, and will earn high profits which will let them pay bigger dividends in future, tend to have low yields. Investors accept less now in the hope of more in future. Companies with poor growth prospects tend to have higher yields.

If a company has a higher than average yield, but still has good prospects of profits growth, the shares may be cheap. And vice versa. You can do a rough check by looking in the Financial Times Actuaries Indices table at the average yields for companies in each major sector of industry.

PRICE EARNINGS RATIOS

If dividend yields offer a crude indication of a company's rating, the price earnings ratio can confirm it. When people talk about a PE ratio of five, the PE of five, five times earnings, or five year's earnings, they are all talking about the same thing – a price earnings ratio of five. (A low rating, incidentally).

The price earnings ratio tells you how many years it will take to make profits after tax and other deductions sufficient to equal the stock market value of the whole company. So a price earnings ratio of five means it will take five years for the company valued at £50 million to make £50 million in net profits after tax. Like the dividend yield, it is an over-simplified measure, but it is the most widely used general piece of market jargon.

In the spring of 1987, the average market price earnings ratio was 17·7, meaning it would have taken the average company 17·7 years to earn net profits equal to the market value of the whole company. Within that average are companies with a PE

61

of five, and companies with a PE of fifty. Once again, the crude clue of whether a share is cheap or dear lies in how far the price earnings ratio deviates from the average for that sort of business.

ASSET VALUES

If you are satisfied that the dividend yield and price earnings ratio on the share of your choice makes sense, next try to find the net asset value. This need not always matter much, and in 1987 most companies were trading at well above asset values. That is fine when the going is good, but asset value can be important in difficult times, or if you are lucky enough to pick a share which receives a takeover bid.

The net asset value reflects the worth of the company if it was sold off, piece by piece. Assets are listed in the balance sheet which is part of the report and accounts each company must send shareholders every year. The main assets of a business are the land, plant, machinery, stocks, cash, investments and similar property that it owns. Deduct from them the debts of a business – loans, tax due, creditors – and what is left is its asset value. Divide that by the number of shares in issue, and you get the net asset value per share.

Working it out can be enormously complicated, and subject to a whole range of subjective opinions. The best asset of all is cash, followed by a good slug of land, the nearer to London and the less vital to the business, the better. Plant and machinery values are suspect – they often fetch poor prices – and stocks may also be worth less than shown in the balance sheet. On the other hand, while a strict view would prompt you to ignore any goodwill in the business, that could prove to be a great boon. If a company hits trouble because it makes toys which no one wants, then the goodwill attached to the brand name may be worthless. But good brand names can be worth a fortune, and sometimes companies will buy a sleepy company just to get hold of well-known names, and introduce new products using the good reputation attached to the old ones.

Obviously asset value does not matter much in a giant like

Marks & Spencer, where no one expects a bid, and no one expects the business to hit such trouble that it has to be sold off bit by bit. But if you are thinking of buying shares in a company with falling profits, asset backing is an important safeguard. Or if you think a bidder may be in the background, strong asset value could be important in the price he will pay. So get a broker to check it for you, or try to hunt it out on an Extel card, or through the *Investors Chronicle*.

MARKET VALUE

The other invaluable piece of jargon to keep in mind is the market value, or capitalization of the company. That is simply stock market-speak for the overall worth of the company as reflected by the share price. You find it out by multiplying the number of shares in issue by their price. *The Times* stock market price table does it for you on Mondays. So does the *Guardian* on Saturdays. And the *Investors Chronicle* company analysis mentions it.

Market value matters because it gives you an idea of whether you are playing with a tiddler or a substantial company. The profits show that as well, of course, but it is surprising how often a reference to the capitalization can demonstrate that bid rumours are completely off-beam once you compare the relative size of target and rumoured bidder.

MARKET SIZE

Market capitalization also gives a clue to another important practical investment standard – the size of the market in the shares. The Stock Exchange now classifies shares as alpha, beta, gamma and delta, according to how large a volume of the shares can be traded freely. There are over 100 alpha stocks. They cover the biggest companies, with a ready market at any time, because several firms will give competing quotations, and will trade large numbers without altering the price. By the time you get down to delta stocks, you could be facing a situation

63

where buying and selling might often be a little difficult. So watch out.

This matters most to the big players, but it is worth keeping in mind when you deal. So long as shares are rising, there will be relatively little problem. But if there should be a setback, ease of dealing will be crucial. The less actively traded shares will suddenly be quoted with wider margins between buying and selling prices (the spread), and it will be hard to trade in more than small quantities without the price shifting against you.

This is one of the reasons why most PEP managers who allow investors to pick from a range of shares confine that range to alpha stocks, from the biggest companies. If you get caught in what is known as a narrow market stock, you could find it hard to sell at any price if the market turns sharply down. And you could easily find it hard to deal without taking a lower price than you had expected. So unless you know what you are doing, and are ready to take a greater risk, stick to bigger companies with three or more market-makers, and stick to the sort of quantities which are comfortably within the size limits you can trade normally. Do not buy 10,000 shares where the market is normally in 5,000. This may seem a terrific idea when prices are rising, but getting out could prove a killer if they fall.

SELLING SHARES

You should certainly treat PEPs as a long-term investment. But you will want to sell at some time. And this is where most investors make their biggest mistake. They get greedy, indulge in extreme wishful-thinking, and hold on too long.

It is easy to think that big losses are what happens to the other fellow. They are not. They could happen to you all too easily. If you are an inexperienced investor, you will be stunned at the speed with which prices can turn against you if the market goes bad. Those who were investing through the great slump of 1973 and 1974 know this only too well. It has inhibited almost all who were playing then, and made them perhaps unduly cautious. But there is nothing worse than getting trapped in a falling market, watching profits which have taken years to build up being wiped out almost by the hour.

In the long-term, the fluctuations of the market have not mattered too much. Anyone who bought in 1972, and sat tight through the slump of '73–'74, would have been doing very nicely ten years later. Even five years later, PEPs would have looked fairly good, provided not too many of the real cripples dotted the portfolio.

So if you are a committed long-term player, with five or ten years to go, and you are ready to sweat through a few tough years (which may not come), you need not worry too much about selling. But if you are retiring in ten years' time, or perhaps five years, and will want your cash then, just when the market is down, tough luck. Then you will wish you had worried about when to sell.

THE STOP LOSS SYSTEM

There is no fool-proof system which gets you out at the top of the market with fat profits. Investing in shares is a risk business – for anyone. Over the years, I have used a system which sets stop loss points as a selling guide. It is not perfect, but it would have saved me a small fortune if I had stuck to it in 1974. I hope it did save a fortune for those who took my investment advice at that time, and did what I said they should, rather than what I did myself.

The system is simple. When you buy any share, set a price at which you will sell it. No one buys a share which they think will go down, but anyone sensible has to admit the possibility. So be realistic. Set the stop loss level between 10 and 25 per cent below the price you pay. Vary it according to how sharply that particular share moves, and your own temperament. Since PEP investment should be long-term, it makes sense to be more patient, and set the stop loss price at a fairly generous margin below the trading price – say 20–25 per cent. So if you buy at 100p, set a stop loss price of 75p. If the share falls to 75p, sell. The price is telling you that you have almost certainly got it wrong, and enough people are selling to suggest that there is something you do not know about. Never lower your stop loss.

All being well, however, your 100p share will rise. As it does, move the stop loss price up behind it. So when it reaches 110p, your stop loss may be 85p. When it hits 125p, your stop loss is 100p. When it reaches 150p, your stop loss may be 125p. And so on. That way, you should keep some profits if the price does turn tail after a good run.

RUNNING PROFITS

Conventional investment wisdom might suggest you sell half of your investment when a share doubles, so that the shares you keep have effectively cost you nothing. Disregard it. If you pick a winner, you want to stick with it. Simply keep trailing your stop loss up behind the price, so that if your 100p share hits 200p, you will sell on a fall to 175p. At this stage, you may feel more relaxed with such a winner. Then, as the price gets higher, you may like to give it a little more leeway. After all, 25 per cent of 200p would be 50p. It might be too generous to set a stop loss of 150p on a share at 200p. But perhaps 160p (a 20 per cent margin) might suit you. Or 170p (a margin of 15 per cent) might be better. The trimmings are up to you. Be sensible. And never lower your stop loss price once you have set it. That way, you wriggle out of the discipline you have imposed upon yourself. Then you will find you never swallow hard and sell, and you end up losing money.

Unfortunately, investors large and small are too ready to indulge their losers, hanging on in the hope of something turning up. They run losses, and sell profitable shares to finance the losers. That may be human nature but it is investment madness.

The stop loss system will prompt you to sell some good shares too soon. No system can get everything right. But over the long-term, it will save you far more money than it costs you. Do it. You can trade as often as you like inside a PEP without losing your tax privileges. Cut your losses, and run your profits, please, please, *please*.

10   The PEP Favourites

There is safety in numbers. The need to keep your PEP intact for a calendar year to qualify for tax savings means that the great PEP marketing push comes towards the end of the year, gathering pace from August onwards. Investors will be inundated with PEP promotions, with luck with added refinements to make PEPs even more attractive.

The first selling campaign in the winter of 1986 and spring of 1987 threw up interesting indicators of what the mass of investors felt about PEPs, and how they prefer to use them. The average PEP investor in the opening phase was 50, paid tax at above standard rate, and tended to put in the full £2,400 in one lot. Men and women found it equally attractive, and perhaps three quarters picked a PEP where the managers chose the shares. A sizeable minority put part of the money in a unit trust, often going for an international spread through a trust specializing in foreign shares. And one PEP customer in four was new to the share world.

Managers and individual investors alike tended to buy shares in big, well-known companies, reflecting a longer term view of investment with an emphasis on safety-first capital growth. The early birds got off to a flying start, enjoying the 25 per cent rise in the UK stock market in the first four months of 1987.

SHARE CHOICES

Any list of shares runs the risk of looking lame and out of touch within weeks, as the stock market moves up and down. It is

67

possible, however, to give broad, general guidance which may help PEP beginners, and offer a rough indication of what to expect in the popular stocks. These notes are purely personal, and are not intended to be share recommendations.

Anything could happen to change the ratings from day to day. That is what investment is about, and why it can be risky. In normal times, though, there are certain companies with broadly unchanging characteristics which may appeal to particular investors. The shares are discussed in no special order of merit, but it does make sense to start with a company every serious investor ought to think about – ICI.

IMPERIAL CHEMICAL INDUSTRIES

The daddy of all British industrial companies, with a wide spread of interests from chemicals to paints to fertilizers, textiles and even petrol stations. New chairman Denys Henderson succeeded the effervescent Sir John Harvey-Jones in 1987, hoping to carry on the good work which has seen ICI placing more emphasis on profit, on speciality chemicals, and on North America. Profits are strongly influenced by currency moves, and ICI benefits particularly when a strong Mark makes West German competitors less able to compete internationally on price.

HANSON TRUST

Lord Hanson in London and Sir Gordon White in America have proved the most effective management team of the decade, with an impressive ability to buy undervalued companies, strip out and sell off the parts they do not want, and earn higher profits from what they keep. Strong profits growth attracts controversy, especially when Hanson bids for another company. Detractors say the group needs to keep buying to generate sufficient growth, and fear it has become too big to keep the forward impetus going at a good pace. Still an enormously effective operation.

68

MARKS & SPENCER

The greatest High Street name, growing more adventurous under chairman Lord Rayner. Caught napping a little in the early eighties by more adventurous competition, but generating massive growth from an unstoppable expansion programme, adding store space and new products.

BRITISH TELECOM

First of the giant privatization issues, Telecom has higher costs than the international competition, and faces the challenge of becoming leaner and fitter. Finding it difficult to adapt to the harder disciplines of competing in the outside world, but sure to benefit from ever-increasing demand for telecommunications equipment and services.

BRITISH GAS

The other privatization giant, initially under-rated, but with a vastly ambitious chairman in Sir Denis Rooke. Profits are influenced crucially by the winter weather (cold weather means more gas sales), but with a solid, safe level of high income. Gas might turn out to be a more aggressive company than expected, with faster growth prospects and greater international appeal. Popular with Japanese investors.

BRITISH AIRWAYS

Off to a flying start once privatized, Airways could achieve strong pre-tax profits growth if all goes well. Higher tax charges mean earnings per share will grow more slowly. Capital costs of new planes are heavy, and risks are high. Airways profits could be threatened by faults in any particular type of aircraft, by higher oil prices, renewed terrorist attacks, and restrictive international rules. A relatively high-risk investment.

GREAT UNIVERSAL STORES

Sleeping giant of the High Street, ruled by the Wolfson family, with a large issue of 'A' non-voting shares. The family is rumoured to be moving towards giving votes to the non-voting shares, opening the way to a possible bid, and to be looking for a new management line of succession. Sir Philip Harris of Harris Queensway has close links. Great Universal is big in mail order and credit reference services, with an excellent record of steady, unbroken growth.

BURTON GROUP

Heavily profit-oriented, led aggressively by controversial chairman Sir Ralph Halpern. The bid for Debenhams department stores attracted adverse comment, but Burton promises great profit opportunities if more successful trading can be generated in old Debenhams stores. Doubts over the pace of change held the shares back in the early part of 1987, but strong profits growth is likely in 1987 and 1988, with a question mark over the group's ability to expand thereafter.

NATIONAL WESTMINSTER, LLOYDS, BARCLAYS, AND MIDLAND

All the clearing banks have been rated low by international standards, and have a good, solid rump of growth in the UK. Fears of international banking crises worry some. So do doubts over the standing of the banks' loans to South America and Africa. Midland has had the hardest time, hit by an unwise attempt to expand in America, but has a highly rated new management team under former Bank of England star Sir Kit McMahon.

70

GEC

Keeper of a legendary cash mountain of well over £1 billion, and Britain's most important electrical giant, GEC appears to have lost its way. Chairman Lord Weinstock is renowned for squeezing cash out of the business, but the group lacks dynamism. Subject to occasional bid rumours, but too large for most to tackle.

BTR

One of the City's favourite growth stocks, with a good spread of industrial interests, developed vigorously by former boss Sir Owen Green. Suffered a setback in failing to take over glass giant Pilkington, with questions beginning to emerge over the need for acquisitions to maintain the pace of growth. Highly respected.

THORN EMI

The entertainments and electrical giant has suffered management problems, and is slowly being whipped into shape by a new team. Opponents suggest it may still lack sufficient drive, but signs of new promise began to emerge in 1987.

P & O

An interesting prospect under the relatively new management of chairman Sir Jeffrey Sterling, one of the best-respected managers in the City, with a strong property background to help the shipping problems.

ASDA-MFI

Many felt the merger of the Asda grocery stores with MFI's cheap furniture warehouses was a mistake, and shunned the shares for 1986. Signs of new vigour began to come through in 1987 with a clearer management direction.

PRUDENTIAL CORPORATION

The insurance giant has been enjoying strong profits growth, supported by a more aggressive attention to cutting out loss-makers. The Pru has been helped by a strong stock market to boost the vast investment reserves, and has made a vigorous move into unit trust management and estate agency.

BAT

The big daddy of the tobacco scene, with immense cigarette interests earning big money outside the UK. Diversification into retailing has been patchy, but a major move into financial services is proving more successful. The shares perpetually look undervalued in relation to other giants.

J. SAINSBURY

The great family grocery group. Highly efficient, with a first-class growth record, it holds few surprises, but continues to prosper.

DEE CORPORATION

A supermarket group built on a series of aggressive acquisitions by Alec Monk, a management ace rather than a retailer. Fast expansion and rationalization has generated good growth, but food retailing is a fiercely competitive market.

TESCO

The appointment of Ian McLaurin as chairman has brought a new life to an old favourite, with a determined move up-market into higher quality groceries with higher profit margins. Evidence of a greater interest in expansion is encouraging.

COATS VIYELLA

The major new force in UK textiles, where a troubled industry is fighting back. Chairman David Alliance is the most impressive of a new breed of textile men, growing fast by buying businesses and making them more efficient.

RIO TINTO-ZINC

The British-controlled worldwide natural resources giant. Profits rise and fall with the cycle of commodity prices, but the group has been displaying new life in 1987. Immensely valuable international assets, with extra spice from recurrent bid rumours.

NEXT

Most innovative of the High Street fashion operators under the brilliant leadership of George Davies. Dodged bid battles for more High Street space by merging with mail order group Grattan. A revolutionary new way of selling by mail order planned for early in 1988. Highly rated, but if the new mail order ideas take off, the future looks even brighter. Great growth opportunities in re-shaping Combined English Stores, bought in May 1987.

TSB

One of the new-issue stars of 1986, the TSB pulled in cash for expansion with the flotation. More highly rated than other

High Street banks, but without their potential international bad debt problems. Growth should be steady, but much depends on how the flotation cash is used.

GLAXO

Enjoyed a soaring share price early in 1987 on international buying sparked by the prospects for new drugs. Highly rated, but successful drugs can earn a fortune around the world.

WELLCOME

Like Glaxo, an early 1987 winner, sparked by hopes for a new anti-AIDS treatment. Much will depend on how that can be developed. Highly rated shares could be vulnerable to investment fashion.

CABLE & WIRELESS

The international telecommunications group is the best investment way into China, where Cable & Wireless is an important operator. The Mercury system is emerging as a serious challenger to the British Telecom monopoly. Long-term growth prospects look bright.

BP

The great British oil giant with vast world muscle. Cash-rich, shrewdly managed, BP must be influenced by the oil price. Long-term, that should rise.

GUINNESS

The share rating has been hit by the controversy over discredited chairman Ernest Saunders and the bitter fight for control of Distillers, the whisky giant. Over the long-term, the prospect of exploiting the resources of Distillers should boost profits, though growth elsewhere is by no means assured.

Warning

Buying and selling shares is a risk business. The best managers will not be able to prevent your investment losing value if the whole market falls.

If in doubt sell out.

Unless you are certain you know what you are doing, always pick the biggest and longest-established PEP manager in preference to anyone else.

Never, ever buy shares from someone you do not know. Never buy shares from a stranger on the telephone. Never sell through a firm you do not know. Never trade with an investment firm with headquarters outside the UK.

Never invest in commodities, or futures. Never believe a no-risk guarantee, or promises of a limited loss.

Never get involved in any form of investment you do not fully understand, no matter how respectable the house which tries to sell it to you.

Never think you know it all.

Good luck.

Index